Best-kept Secrets of the Women's Institute

SOUPS

Grace Mulligan & Dilwen Phillips

First published in Great Britain by Simon & Schuster UK Ltd, 2002
A CBS Company

Copyright © this compilation WI Enterprises Ltd 2002. All rights reserved.

Simon & Schuster UK Ltd
Africa House
64–78 Kingsway
London
WC2B 6AH

The right of Grace Mulligan and Dilwen Phillips to be identified as the Authors of this Work has been asserted by

them in accordance with sections 77 and 78 of the Copyright, Designs and Patents Act, 1988.

5 7 9 10 8 6

Design and typesetting: **Fiona Andreanelli**
Food photography: **Steve Baxter**
Home economist: **Sara Buenfeld**
Stylist for food photography: **Liz Belton**
Editor: **Deborah Savage**
Printed and bound in China/Hong Kong/Singapore/Italy

ISBN 0 74322 112 5

CONTENTS

INTRODUCTION

To the tune of '**Food, Glorious Food**', from the musical Oliver, sing '**soup, glorious soup, hot sausage and mustard**'!

Coming from Scotland, Grace thinks soup is pretty special. It will often lift your spirits on a dreary day or even on a sunny one if you aren't feeling special yourself. The stories of Jewish mothers who cure everything with chicken soup have something to them!

The soups Dilwen's mother made were from home-grown vegetables, herbs and meat in season and, when needed, dried pulses and home-cured ham and bacon. They certainly did not have available the range of ingredients that are in this book. She still recalls the delightful flavour of summer vegetable and chicken soup with parsley and marjoram. Soup is still important in her household, taken mainly as a light lunch, and her grandchildren enjoy a mug of puréed soup. She finds this is an excellent way of getting them to eat vegetables they might otherwise reject and the soup colours are appealing

It's depressing, however, that so many people turn to cans or packets when they think of having soup. Often, one look at the ingredients list will tell you a sad tale of artificial flavours, starches and E numbers.

Hopefully the tasty, user-friendly recipes in this book will tempt you to sample the delights and flavours of our home-made soups.

INGREDIENTS FOR SOUPS

Anyone who can cut up fresh vegetables can make soup and you do not have to spend all morning doing it. If you are really pressed for time, buy a packet of chopped fresh vegetables. Just check that they are really fresh and moist. Almost any vegetable can be made into soup and this is a great way to use up any odd vegetables that are left in the fridge at the end of the week.

Pulses, such as lentils, split peas, dried green peas and chick-peas can make soups really substantial and filling and are a good source of protein, which is particularly helpful to the vegetarian. Don't forget also what a delicious and useful addition potatoes are. White floury potatoes, which break down during cooking, not only add their flavour but are good natural thickeners for soups. Waxy potatoes, on the other hand, if they are peeled and cubed, give a soup good texture. We underestimate potatoes. Just think of the glamorous-sounding French soup, vichyssoise. This is just a poshed-up version of good old leek and potato soup, served chilled.

Butter or oil is used in these recipes to soften onions and other vegetables. This gives a good flavour but there is no reason why a low-fat spread should not be used (though these do not give good results when browning is required because of the water they contain).

Herbs are important to soups, not just for flavouring but also for their colour. If you have your own herb patch, you can enjoy parsley, mint, chives, coriander and sorrel very cheaply. I often think we are too mean with herbs: when you hear your favourite chef say 'stir in a small handful of parsley', he really means a handfull! Fresh herbs have been used throughout this book; if you are substituting dried herbs, reduce the quantity by half.

Meat or poultry can be the basis of really hearty soups that are a meal in themselves, with some good bread.

TECHNIQUES FOR MAKING SOUPS

As a general rule, for all soups use a minimum of 450-675 g (1–1½ lb) of ingredients to every 1 litre (1¾ pints) of stock, with the main ingredient(s) predominating. About 200 ml (7 fl oz) of soup per person is sufficient as a starter but allow at least 300 ml (½ pint) per serving if the soup is to act as a light lunch – perhaps more for a main course.

The terms '**sauté**', '**sweat**' and '**soften**' are all used in recipes to describe initial cooking of onion or vegetables in oil or butter. Basically, they all mean the same thing: the technique softens the onion and/or other vegetables and develops the flavour but without caramelising them (that is, without browning). Thus, a gentle heat and a covered pan (so the steam is retained to help soften the vegetables) should be used and you should shake the pan frequently to prevent the contents from sticking on the bottom, and browning as a consequence. '**Frying**' on the other hand means softening and colouring onions, other vegetables and/or meat. This process adds the flavours developed by caramelising as well as colour to the finished dish.

Many soups in this book have been puréed to give a smooth texture.

Liquidisers, food processors and hand-held 'stick' blenders will all purée soups quite satisfactorily. A hand-held blender is perhaps the easiest to use because you can purée the soup still in the saucepan, saving on washing up. Liquidisers produce the smoothest purée whilst a food processor will also produce a perfectly good result if the soup is processed in short bursts. You can also produce a smooth texture using a food mill or by rubbing the mixture through a sieve but both methods are time-consuming and leave you with equipment that is difficult to clean.

Most soups can be frozen and, if you are just cooking for one or two, you can have real instant soup in your freezer by making quantities for four or more – which takes just the same time – and freezing portions. Just remember to label and date your containers and use them within two months.

Dairy products such as cheese can be problematic when frozen but this should not affect these recipes; as long as soups are reheated fairly gently but thoroughly they should be fine; any separation of fat in soups containing cheese or cream can be dispersed with a good whisking.

Microwave soups can save time, but only if you cook a small quantity (no more than four portions), if the vegetables are finely chopped or grated and boiling stock is added. Use a large, round container for cooking microwave soups; bear in mind also that meat will not tenderise in the microwave. Within these limitations, however, you can have a good soup ready in just a few minutes.

The general method for cooking soup in the microwave is to melt the butter first and then soften the onions in the butter on full power for 4 minutes. Allow another 4 minutes to sauté the vegetables. Add half the recommended quantity of boiling stock to the vegetables and cook on full power for 5 minutes. Stir and cook for a further 5 minutes or until the vegetables are cooked. Add the remaining boiling stock and continue as for conventional cooking.

There are many easy ways to make a soup look extra special. It can be as simple as scattering a few chopped herbs or a few crunchy croûtons. Croûtons are made by frying cubed bread in a little oil until brown and crisp. You could also consider larger pieces of bread called croûtes. They are either grilled or baked. If the bread is spread lightly with a layer of garlic butter prior to baking it is even better. Grated cheese, toasted on thin slices of french bread, is the classic topping for French Onion Soup, as on page 54, but this is also a nice idea for tomato and fish soups. You could also consider little puff-pastry shapes, baked, for special occasions.

Another suitable finishing touch is to swirl a spoonful of cream, crème fraîche or natural or greek-style yoghurt into each serving of a smooth soup.

Whether you take your soup whizzed to smooth perfection with a hand-blender in a favourite mug for a quick lunch or served in a china bowl on a nicely laid table, do enjoy our recipes and then use them as the basis for trying out your own ideas. In no time at all you will be making up your own soup recipes.

We would like to thank friends and colleagues for sharing their recipes and ideas with us and hope you enjoy cooking and eating the soups.

Grace Mulligan & Dilwen Phillips

MEASUREMENTS

OVEN TEMPERATURES

Gas Mark	Electric (°C)	Fan oven (°C)
	80	60
	90	70
	100	80
E	110	90
I	120	100
I	130	110
I	140	120
2	150	130
3	160	140
3	170	150
4	180	160
5	190	170
6	200	180
6	210	190
7	220	200
8	230	210
9	240	220
9	250	230

NOTE: These temperatures are equivalent settings rather than exact conversions of degrees of heat.

VOLUME MEASURES

$1/4$ teaspoon	1.25 ml
$1/2$ teaspoon	2.5 ml
I teaspoon	5 ml
2 teaspoons	10 ml
I tablespoon	15 ml

NOTE: When teaspoons/tablespoons are used for measuring dry ingredients, these should be rounded (as much of the ingredient above as in the bowl of the spoon). Measuring spoons should be filled only so the top surface is level.

VOLUME MEASURES

Imperial (fluid ounces/pints)	Metric (millilitres/litres)
I fl oz	25 ml
2 fl oz	50 ml
3 fl oz	80 ml
4 fl oz	115 ml
5 fl oz/$1/4$ pint	150 ml
6 fl oz	175 ml
7 fl oz	200 ml
8 fl oz	225 ml
9 fl oz	250 ml
10 fl oz/$1/2$ pint	300 ml
11 fl oz	325 ml
12 fl oz	350 ml
13 fl oz	375 ml
14 fl oz	400 ml
15 fl oz/$3/4$ pint	425 ml
16 fl oz	450 ml
17 fl oz	475 ml
18 fl oz	500 ml
19 fl oz	550 ml
20 fl oz/1 pint	575 ml
$1 1/4$ pints	700 ml
$1 1/2$ pints	850 ml
$1 3/4$ pints	I litre
2 pints	1.1 litres
$2 1/4$ pints	1.3 litres
$2 1/2$ pints	1.4 litres
$2 3/4$ pints	1.6 litres
3 pints	1.7 litres
$3 1/4$ pints	2 litres

NOTE: The measurements are equivalents, not exact conversions. Always follow either the imperial or the metric measures and do not mix the two in one recipe.

WEIGHT MEASURES

Imperial (ounces/pounds)	Metric (grams/kilograms)
I oz	25 g
2 oz	50 g
3 oz	80 g
4 oz	115 g
5 oz	150 g
6 oz	175 g
7 oz	200 g
8 oz	225 g
9 oz	250 g
10 oz	275 g
11 oz	300 g
12 oz	350 g
13 oz	375 g
14 oz	400 g
15 oz	425 g
16 oz	450 g
I lb I oz	475 g
I lb 2 oz	500 g
I lb 3 oz	525 g
I lb 4 oz	550 g
I lb 5 oz	600 g
I lb 6 oz	625 g
I lb 7 oz	650 g
I lb 8 oz	675 g
2 lb 8 oz	900 g
3 lb 8 oz	1.3 kg
3 lb 5 oz	1.5 kg

SPRING SOUPS

SERVES 4
PREPARATION TIME:
30 minutes + 20 minutes cooking
FREEZING: not recommended

The name '**chowder**' comes from the French *chaudière*, a large cooking pan. Traditionally, chowder was made with belly pork but we have substituted bacon to reduce the cooking time. Although classed as a soup, chowder is more of a meal in itself. There are endless variations because you can use any combination of available fish and vegetables to suit your taste.

125 g (4 oz) rindless streaky bacon, chopped
1 large onion, chopped
350 g (12 oz) potatoes, chopped
1 carrot, chopped
1 small parsnip, chopped
425 ml (15 fl oz) fish stock (page 75)
8 scallops
juice of 1 lemon
25 g (1 oz) plain flour
575 ml (1 pint) milk
salt and pepper
15 ml (1 tablespoon) chopped fresh parsley, to garnish

1 Heat a large pan and fry the bacon over a low heat, without any added oil, until the fat is released.
2 Add the onion and soften until transparent.
3 Add the remaining vegetables and the stock. Bring to the boil and then reduce the heat and simmer for 15–20 minutes, or until the vegetables are cooked.
4 Meanwhile, clean the scallops by removing all the black parts. Set the corals aside. Roughly chop the white flesh and sprinkle with lemon juice.
5 Blend the flour with a little of the milk until smooth. Add the remainder of the milk and then pour the mixture into the vegetables Stir until the soup has thickened.
6 Add the scallops and simmer for 5 minutes.
7 Add the corals and simmer for 2 minutes.
8 Adjust the seasoning and serve sprinkled with parsley.

SCALLOP CHOWDER

SERVES 4
PREPARATION TIME: 20 minutes + 20 minutes cooking
FREEZING: recommended before adding cheese and croûtons

CREAM OF CELERY, APPLE & STILTON SOUP

The sharpness of the apple counteracts the richness of the cheese in this unusual soup.

25 g (I oz) butter
I onion, chopped
3 celery sticks, chopped
15 ml (I tablespoon) plain flour
575 ml (I pint) vegetable stock (page 75)
150 ml ($^1/_4$ pint) white wine
300 ml ($^1/_2$ pint) milk
I bay leaf
2.5 ml ($^1/_2$ teaspoon) dried mixed herbs
I cooking apple, peeled and chopped
80 g (3 oz) Stilton cheese, finely diced
salt and freshly ground black pepper
croûtons (page 23), to serve

1 Heat the butter in a large saucepan and sauté the onion and celery for 2–3 minutes, until softened but not browned.
2 Stir in the flour and cook for a further minute. Gradually add the stock and wine. Bring to the boil, stirring, until thickened.
3 Add the milk, bay leaf, herbs and apple. Bring back to the boil, cover and simmer for 20 minutes.
4 Meanwhile, make the croûtons (page 23) and keep them warm.
5 Remove the bay leaf from the soup, allow to cool slightly, and then liquidise.
6 Return to the pan, add the cheese and heat gently until melted.
7 Season to taste, Serve each bowlful with a few croûtons on top.

SERVES 4
PREPARATION AND COOKING TIME: 25 minutes
FREEZING: recommended after step 5

CHEESY CAULIFLOWER & BROCCOLI SOUP

The addition of walnuts gives this soup an interesting crunchy texture.

15 ml (I tablespoon) sunflower oil
I small onion, chopped
350 g (12 oz) cauliflower florets
350 g (12 oz) broccoli florets
1.1 litres (2 pints) vegetable stock (page 75)
25 g (I oz) plain flour
30 ml (2 tablespoons) milk
25 g (I oz) walnuts, chopped
2.5 ml ($^1/_2$ teaspoon) freshly grated nutmeg
200 g (7 oz) cream cheese
115 g (4 oz) mature Cheddar cheese, grated
salt and pepper
croûtons, to serve (page 23)

1 Heat the oil in a large pan and soften the onion.
2 Add the cauliflower, broccoli and stock. Cook for 5–10 minutes; the cauliflower and broccoli should be tender but not soft.
3 Meanwhile, make the croûtons (page 23) and keep them warm.
4 Blend together the vegetable stock, flour and milk and add to the cauliflower and broccoli mixture.
5 Add the walnuts and nutmeg.
6 Add the two cheeses and stir the soup over a gentle heat until the cheese is well blended and the soup has thickened.
7 Adjust the seasoning and serve each bowlful with a few croûtons.

SERVES 4
PREPARATION & COOKING TIME: 50 minutes
FREEZING: not recommended

CULLEN SKINK

The word **skink** means '**stock**' or '**broth**'; Cullen is the name of a fishing village in Aberdeenshire. This is a traditional Scottish soup and is a meal in itself. The authentic recipe uses Finnan haddock (a particular type of smoked haddock) but, if you can't get this, choose a haddock that is smoked but not dyed. And remember that fish should not be cooked for too long, otherwise it becomes tough. Two pans are needed for this soup unless you cook the potatoes beforehand.

350 g (12 oz) Finnan haddock
1 onion, chopped
1 small carrot, chopped
4 whole cloves
850 ml (1½ pints) water or fish stock (page 75)
575 ml (1 pint) milk
450 g (1 lb) potatoes, chopped coarsely
25 g (1 oz) butter
salt and freshly ground black pepper
chopped fresh parsley, to garnish

1 Put the haddock, onion, carrot and cloves in a pan and pour on the water or stock. Bring gently to the boil and simmer for no more than 5 minutes.
2 Remove the fish and, when cool enough to handle, remove the skin and bones. Return the skin and bones to the pan, add the milk and continue cooking over a low heat.
   Flake the haddock flesh.
3 Meanwhile, cook the potatoes in boiling, salted water until tender. Drain, leaving a little water in the pan.
4 Mash the potatoes with the butter.
5 Strain the milky stock from the fish bones. Blend into the mashed potatoes until the mixture is smooth. Add the flaked haddock.
6 Reheat the soup without boiling, but be careful not to overcook it.
7 Adjust the seasoning and serve garnished with chopped parsley.

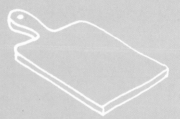
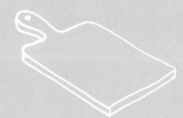

SERVES 4
PREPARATION TIME:
30 minutes + 20 minutes cooking
FREEZING: recommended

Potato soup is **delicious** on its own and is also a good base for a number of variations.

POTATO SOUP

50 g (2 oz) butter
450 g (1 lb) potatoes, chopped
1 large onion, chopped
15 g ('/₂ oz) plain flour
850 ml (1'/₂ pints) vegetable stock (page 75)
a bouquet garni
about 300 ml ('/₂ pint) milk
salt, pepper and freshly grated nutmeg
chopped fresh parsley, to garnish

1 Melt the butter in a large pan and sweat the potatoes and onion, covered, for 10–15 minutes. Stir regularly and do not let them brown.
2 Sprinkle the flour on to the vegetables and mix well.
3 Add the stock and bouquet garni and stir well to make sure the flour is well blended. Bring back to the boil, reduce the heat and simmer for 15–20 minutes, until the vegetables are cooked.
4 Purée the soup. Return it to the pan and reheat gently.
5 Add enough of the milk to make the soup the consistency of thick cream.
6 Season with salt, pepper and two gratings of nutmeg. Serve sprinkled with chopped parsley.

VARIATIONS:
Add 2–3 stalks of lemon grass, cut into 2.5 cm (1- inch) pieces, with the potatoes and onion.
After the soup has been puréed, add one of the following:

115 g (4 oz) home-cooked ham, cubed
115 g (4 oz) bacon, grilled and chopped
115 g (4 oz) salami or other sausage, sliced or cubed
115 g (4 oz) broccoli florets, broad beans or peas, blanched
115 g (4 oz) belly pork, roasted and cubed

SERVES 4
PREPARATION TIME:
20 minutes + 1 hour cooking
FREEZING: not recommended

Grace says: 'barley was always included in the soup I had at home when I was young. I love the texture it gives to soup and I'm glad to see it's making a comeback. Not long ago in a restaurant I had a risotto made with barley instead of rice, which perhaps should have been called a "**barlotto**"!'

BARLEY BROTH WITH CHICKEN

15 ml (1 tablespoon) oil
4 chicken drumsticks
1 onion, chopped finely
1 carrot, chopped small
1 celery stick, chopped small
1 leek, sliced finely
2 potatoes, chopped small
1.1 litres (2 pints) chicken stock (page 77)
40 g (1½ oz) pearl barley
1 fresh thyme sprig and 1 bay leaf
60 ml (4 tablespoons) chopped fresh parsley
salt and pepper

1 In a large pan, heat the oil and fry the drumsticks hard until they are well browned all over. Use tongs to remove the chicken to a plate and set this aside. Lower the heat a little.

2 Now add the onion, carrot, celery, leek and potato to the pan and sweat the vegetables, covered, shaking the pan occasionally, for about 10 minutes; you may need to add a little more oil.

3 Then add everything else, including the chicken but reserving 1 tablespoon of chopped parsley. Bring to the boil and then reduce the heat to a simmer.

5 Cook for about 2 hours. Stir often.

6 Remove the chicken to a plate and fish out the bay leaf and sprig of thyme. When the chicken is cool enough to handle, separate the meat from the skin and bones. Chop it and return it to the broth.

7 Adjust the seasoning and serve hot, with the rest of the parsley scattered on top.

RED PEPPER & GOAT'S CHEESE SOUP *pictured opposite*

SERVES 6
PREPARATION TIME:
20 minutes + 20 minutes cooking
FREEZING: recommended after step 3

2 onions, chopped
1.7 litres (3 pints) vegetable stock (page 75)
60 ml (4 tablespoons) dry white wine
8 red peppers, chopped coarsely
1 large cooking apple, cored
and chopped coarsely
5 ml (1 teaspoon) chopped fresh basil
150 g (5 oz) goat's cheese, rind removed
salt and pepper
6 fresh basil leaves, to garnish

This creamy soup is a **delicious blend of flavours** enriched by the addition of goat's cheese. Everyone who's tried it agrees with Dilwen that it is moreish.

1 In a large pan, boil the onions in a little of the stock until the stock has evaporated and the onions are beginning to caramelise.
2 Add the wine, remaining stock, peppers, apple and basil. Cook over a low heat for 20 minutes.
3 Liquidise the soup. Return to the pan and reheat. Adjust the seasoning.
4 Add the cheese and whisk over a gentle heat until blended.
5 Serve each portion garnished with a basil leaf.

BUTTERNUT SQUASH & APPLE SOUP

SERVES 4
PREPARATION TIME:
15 minutes + 35 minutes cooking
FREEZING: recommended

15 ml (1 tablespoon) oil
1 onion, sliced thinly
5 ml (1 teaspoon) curry powder
2 eating apples, peeled, cored and chopped
1 medium butternut squash, peeled,
de-seeded and chopped
1 litre (1³/₄ pints) vegetable stock (page 75)
salt and pepper
croûtons, to garnish (page 23)

Butternut squash is imported and, unlike the squashes grown in this country, is available in winter and spring. The combination of flavours gives a delicious soup.

1 Heat the oil in a large pan, add the onion and cook for 4–5 minutes, until softened but not browned.
2 Stir in the curry powder and the apple and cook for 2 minutes.
3 Add the squash and stock. Bring to the boil and then reduce the heat. Simmer for 15–20 minutes.
4 Meanwhile, make the croûtons (page 23) and keep warm.
5 Remove from the heat and leave to cool briefly. Purée the soup. Adjust the seasoning and then reheat gently. Thin the soup with a little more stock, if necessary. Serve with a few croûtons sprinkled on each bowl.

SERVES 4
PREPARATION TIME: 25 minutes + 15 minutes cooking
FREEZING: not recommended

CREAMY SPINACH & ALMOND SOUP

15 ml (1 tablespoon) oil
1 onion, chopped
1 potato, chopped
225 g (8 oz) frozen young leaf spinach
575 ml (1 pint) chicken stock (page 77)
a pinch of freshly grated nutmeg (optional)
35 g (1½ oz) ground almonds
salt and freshly ground black pepper
150 ml (5 fl oz) carton of single cream, to serve
15 ml (1 tablespoon) flaked almonds, toasted, to garnish

1 In a large saucepan, heat the oil. Add the onion and potato and sauté for 10 minutes, stirring occasionally. Do not allow to brown.
2 Add the spinach and sauté for a further 5 minutes.
3 Add the stock, nutmeg (if using) and seasoning; bring to the boil, cover and simmer for 15 minutes.
4 Liquidise half the soup until nearly smooth. Return to the pan and stir in the ground almonds and two-thirds of the cream. Reheat gently but do not allow to boil.
5 Ladle into individual bowls and serve with swirls of the remaining cream and a scattering of toasted flaked almonds.

SERVES 6
PREPARATION TIME: 15 minutes + 20 minutes cooking
FREEZING: not recommended

CURRIED BANANA SOUP

This unusual soup is surprisingly easy and delicious.

25 g (1 oz) butter
115 g (4 oz) onion, chopped finely
5 ml (1 teaspoon) good-quality curry powder or paste
850 ml (1½ pints) chicken stock (page 77)
350 g (12 oz) ripe and perfect bananas, chopped
30 ml (2 tablespoons) lemon juice
salt and pepper
150 ml carton of single cream, to serve

1 Melt the butter in a roomy pan and sweat the onion, covered. Shake the pan occasionally over a moderate heat for 5 about minutes. Do not let the onion brown or burn.
2 Now sprinkle the curry powder or paste over the onion and cook for about a minute, stirring all the time.
3 Add the stock, bananas, lemon juice and salt to taste. Bring to the boil and then reduce the heat to a simmer and leave to cook for about 15–20 minutes.
4 Remove from the heat and purée until smooth.
5 Stir in the cream, reheat gently without boiling and season to taste. Serve at once.

SERVES 4
PREPARATION & COOKING TIME: 40 minutes
FREEZING: not recommended

CREAM OF WATERCRESS SOUP

25 g (1 oz) butter
1 onion, chopped
2 bunches of watercress, washed and chopped roughly
40 (1¹/₂ oz) plain flour
850 ml (1¹/₂ pints) chicken stock (page 77)
150 ml carton of cream
salt, freshly ground pepper and freshly grated nutmeg

1 In a large pan, melt the butter and soften the onion, without browning.
2 Add the watercress, reserving a few leaves to garnish. Cover with the lid and allow to sweat for 10 minutes.
3 Stir in the flour and cook for a minute; add the stock, stirring well to ensure the flour is well blended, and then bring to the boil.
4 Reduce to a simmer and cook for 5 minutes.
5 Allow the soup to cool slightly and then purée it.
6 Return the soup to a clean pan and stir in the cream. Season with salt, pepper and nutmeg to taste.
7 Reheat gently without boiling and serve garnished with the reserved watercress leaves.

SERVES 6
PREPARATION: 10 minutes + 20 minutes cooking
FREEZING: recommended

BRAZIL NUT & LEMON SOUP

This has been a great favourite of Grace's since someone sent her the recipe from a cruise liner! It is a good way to use up any leftover Christmas nuts. The soup is light and fresh in flavour, quite spring-like and not at all filling.

25 g (1 oz) butter
1 onion, sliced
1.1 litres (2 pints) chicken stock (page 77)
115 g (4 oz) shelled brazil nuts, chopped roughly
grated zest of 1 lemon
90 ml (6 tablespoons) single cream
salt and freshly ground black pepper

1 In a large pan, melt the butter and sweat the onion, covered, for about 15 minutes. Shake the pan often.
2 Add the stock, nuts and lemon zest. Season lightly, cover and simmer for about 20 minutes.
3 Remove from the heat, allow to cool slightly and purée the mixture. I prefer to use a hand-blender or a food processor rather than a liquidiser for this, as I like to leave some of the texture of the nuts.
4 Reheat the soup, stir in the cream and check the seasoning before serving hot.

SERVES 4
PREPARATION TIME:
20 minutes + 15 minutes cooking
FREEZING: recommended after step 3

This soup can be puréed but Dilwen likes the crunchiness of the celery. It is the ideal starter for a meal with a substantial main course to follow, because it is light and fresh-tasting, from the slight sharpness of the lemon.

25 g (1 oz) butter
2 onions, chopped finely
80 g (3 oz) carrots, grated
80 g (3 oz) celery, very finely chopped
2 lemons
15 g (½ oz) plain flour
1.1 litres (2 pints) chicken stock (page 77)
2 bay leaves
salt and pepper
150 ml carton of single cream, to serve

1 Melt the butter in a large pan. Sweat the onion, carrot and celery, covered and shaking the pan from time to time, over a low heat for 10–15 minutes, without browning.
2 Remove some strips of lemon zest (with a zester if available) and reserve for the garnish. Grate the remaining zest from both lemons and squeeze out the juice.
3 Add the flour to the vegetables in the pan, mix well and cook briefly. Stir in the chicken stock, making sure the flour has blended smoothly. Add the bay leaves and grated lemon zest.
4 Cook for 15 minutes or until the vegetables are soft.
5 Remove the bay leaves and add 20 ml (4 teaspoons) of the lemon juice. Adjust the seasoning and add more lemon juice to taste if necessary.
6 Stir in the cream and reheat gently, without boiling. Serve at once, garnished with the reserved strips of lemon zest.

CREAM OF LEMON SOUP

SERVES 8
PREPARATION:
20 minutes + 30 minutes cooking
FREEZING: recommended

No book on soups would be complete without cabbage soup. Cabbage is available all year round. Add a variety of green vegetables in season and flavourings to suit your own taste. Dilwen finds this is an excellent way of using a glut of cabbage, courgettes, fennel and spinach from the garden.

6 large onions, chopped
2 large green peppers, chopped
1 head of celery, chopped
1 green cabbage, shredded
2 x 400 g cans of tomatoes
40 g can of tomato paste
vegetable stock (page 75)

FLAVOURINGS
(use some of the following):
1 lemon grass stem
3 garlic cloves, crushed
7.5 cm (3-inch) piece of fresh root ginger, grated
10 ml (2 teaspoons) caraway seeds
dried mixed herbs.
2 chillies, de-seeded and sliced thinly

1 Put all the ingredients into a large pan, such as a preserving pan.
2 Add enough boiling stock to come halfway up the vegetables.
3 Add any flavourings you like, bring to the boil and simmer until the vegetables are tender, about 30 minutes.
4 Cool and freeze in individual portions.

NOTE: Other vegetables can also be added to provide variety; try courgettes, beansprouts, fennel or spinach.

CABBAGE SOUP

SERVES 4
PREPARATION TIME: 15 minutes + 15 minutes cooking
FREEZING: recommended before adding the yoghurt

CARROT & CORIANDER SOUP

This soup could be cooked in the microwave.

25 g (1 oz) butter
1 onion, chopped
1 garlic clove, crushed
25 g (1 oz) plain flour
1 litre (1³/₄ pints) chicken stock (page 77)
450 g (1 lb) carrots, grated
10 ml (2 teaspoons) chopped fresh coriander
salt and pepper
60 ml (4 tablespoons) natural yoghurt, to serve

1 Melt the butter in a pan and soften the onion and garlic.
2 Blend in the flour and then add the stock gradually, stirring all the time over a low heat.
3 Add the carrots and coriander. Bring the soup to the boil and then let it simmer for 15 minutes.
4 Remove the pan from the heat and adjust the seasoning.
5 Divide between four bowls and a swirl some yoghurt into each.

SERVES 6–8
PREPARATION TIME: 30 minutes + 30 minutes cooking
FREEZING: recommended

CURRIED VEGETABLE SOUP WITH COCONUT MILK

Do not be put off by the long list of ingredients in this soup – it is so unusual and delicious that it is worth making the effort!

50 g (2 oz) butter
seeds from 3 green cardamom pods (see Note)
5 ml (1 teaspoon) each ground coriander and ground cumin
a large pinch of ground turmeric
2 large carrots, chopped
2 leeks, chopped
3 thick stems of lemon grass, peeled and chopped
225 g (8 oz) celeriac, chopped, or 4 thick celery sticks, chopped
1 fat garlic clove, grated coarsely
a knob of fresh root ginger, grated
400 ml can of coconut milk
1.1 litres (2 pints) chicken stock (page 77)
salt and pepper

1 In a large pan, melt the butter and fry the cardamom pods, coriander, cumin and turmeric. Keep the heat low.
2 Add all the vegetables, including the lemon grass, garlic and ginger, and stir well. Put the lid on and sweat them for a few minutes, shaking often.
2 Stir in the remaining ingredients. Bring to the boil and then reduce the heat and leave to simmer until the vegetables are soft.
3 Reduce to a purée. Pour through a nylon sieve into a clean pan.
4 Reheat, adjust the seasoning to suit you and serve hot.

NOTE: To prepare the cardamom pods, roughly crush with the end of a rolling pin or with a pestle and mortar and extract the seeds.

SERVES 4
PREPARATION & COOKING TIME: 40 minutes
FREEZING: recommended for soup (not croûtons) after step 5

CREAM OF MUSHROOM SOUP WITH CROÛTONS

50 g (2 oz) butter
450 g (1 lb) mushrooms, chopped finely
1 onion, chopped finely
1 garlic clove, crushed (optional)
25 g (1 oz) plain flour
450 ml (16 fl oz) milk
450 ml (16 fl oz) vegetable or chicken stock (page 75 or 77)
150 ml carton of single cream
salt and pepper

FOR THE CROÛTONS:
1 thick slice of day-old white bread, crusts cut off, cubed
oil, for frying

1 In a large pan, melt the butter. Sauté the mushrooms in the butter, with the onion and garlic, if using.
2 Add the flour and stir in well. Cook briefly. Add the milk and stock; stir well to make sure the flour is completely blended.
3 Bring to the boil and simmer for 15 minutes.
4 Meanwhile, make the croûtons. Heat the oil and fry the cubes of bread over a brisk heat for a few minutes, until browned on all sides. Remove with a slotted spoon and place on kitchen paper to drain. Keep warm.
5 Cool the soup a little and add the cream. Liquidise for a smoother finish.
6 For a thicker soup, add a little cornflour or arrowroot, blended with a little water.
7 Reheat the soup gently but do not allow it to boil. Check the seasoning and serve at once, with the croûtons.

SERVES 4–5
PREPARATION TIME: 10 minutes + 10 minutes cooking
FREEZING: not recommended

SALMON & DILL SOUP

Janet Melvin says: '**This is a lovely soup for a special occasion, rich and creamy and one to impress your friends**.'

25 g (1 oz) butter
1 onion, chopped
50 g (2 oz) plain flour
850 ml (1½ pints) fish stock (page 75)
450 g (1 lb) fresh tomatoes, skinned and roughly chopped, or a 400 g can of tomatoes
425 g (15 oz) can of red salmon, drained, the skin and bones removed, flesh flaked
15 ml (1 tablespoon) chopped fresh dill
10 ml (2 teaspoons) lemon juice
150 ml carton of double cream
80 ml (3 fl oz) white wine
salt and freshly ground black pepper
fresh dill sprigs, to garnish

1 Melt the butter in a large saucepan, add the onion and sauté for 5 minutes, until just soft. Add the flour and cook, stirring, for a further minute.
3 Stir in the fish stock, making sure the flour is well blended. Then add the tomatoes and half the flaked salmon. Bring to the boil, cover and simmer for 10 minutes, stirring occasionally.
4 Allow to cool slightly and then purée until smooth.
5 Return the soup to the pan and add the remaining salmon, and the dill, lemon juice, cream and wine. Season to taste.
6 Reheat gently but do not allow to boil. Serve garnished with sprigs of dill.

SERVES 4
PREPARATION TIME:
25 minutes + 15 minutes cooking
FREEZING: recommended after step 3

This is a substantial, satisfying soup with a very good flavour and is ideal for lunch on a cold day. For extra taste, use a thick slice of the best quality ham you can get.

15 ml (I tablespoon) oil
3 leeks, sliced
175 g (6 oz) frozen peas
850 ml (1½ pints) chicken stock (page 77)
175 g (6 oz) ham, cut into chunks
30 ml (2 tablespoons) chopped fresh mint
150 ml carton of double cream, to serve

1 Heat the oil in a large saucepan and sauté the leeks for 8 minutes, stirring occasionally. Add the peas and stock and bring to the boil.
2 Cover and simmer for 15 minutes.
3 Cool slightly and then purée until coarsely blended.
4 Return to the pan, stir in the ham and chopped mint and heat through.
5 Serve in individual bowls, with a swirl of cream.

GREEN PEA, HAM & LEEK SOUP

SERVES 4
PREPARATION & COOKING TIME:
25 minutes
FREEZING: not recommended

This is a Chinese soup, hence the use of chicken rather than fish stock. Make the stock in the way described on page 77 but omit the herbs and add a piece of fresh root ginger about 2.5 cm (1 inch) long, peeled and grated, and 15 ml (1 tablespoon) of soy sauce.

TOFU & SEAFOOD SOUP

12 medium-size prawns,
cut in half lengthways
225 g (8 oz) skinless, boneless white fish,
thinly sliced
175 g (6 oz) tofu
5 ml (1 teaspoon) cornflour
5 ml (1 teaspoon) sesame oil
50 g (2 oz) carrots, sliced thinly
4 thin slices of fresh root ginger
575 ml (1 pint) chicken stock (page 77)
salt and freshly ground black pepper
2 spring onions, cut lengthways in 2.5 cm
(1-inch) pieces, to garnish

1 Sprinkle the prawns, fish and tofu with the cornflour and oil and season with pepper.
2 In a large pan, cook the carrot and ginger slices in the stock for 10 minutes.
3 Add the prawns, fish and tofu and simmer for a further 2–3 minutes or until the fish is cooked.
4 Adjust the seasoning and serve garnished with the spring onions.

SUMMER SOUPS

TOMATO & PLUM SOUP *pictured opposite*

SERVES 4
PREPARATION TIME:
20 minutes + 25 minutes cooking
FREEZING: recommended

15 ml (1 tablespoon) olive oil
1 onion, chopped
450 g (1 lb) red plums, stoned
450 g (1 lb) tomatoes, chopped
300 ml (½ pint) tomato juice
575 ml (1 pint) chicken stock (page 77)
fresh thyme sprig
salt and pepper
15 ml (1 tablespoon) chopped
fresh parsley
or 60 ml (4 tablespoons) crème fraîche

A sharp, bright red soup that is equally as good served hot or chilled.

1 In a large pan, heat the oil and soften the onion, without browning.
2 Add all the other ingredients, except the chopped parsley and the crème fraîche.
3 Bring to the boil and simmer for 25 minutes or until the plums are soft.
4 Cool slightly and then remove the thyme sprig and liquidise until smooth.
5 Check the seasoning and then gently reheat or chill, as your prefer. Serve with a dollop of crème fraîche on each portion or, alternatively, sprinkle each serving with chopped parsley.

BORSHCH

SERVES 4
PREPARATION TIME:
15 minutes + 1 hour cooking
FREEZING: recommended

1 large onion, grated
1 large potato, grated
450 g (1lb) raw beetroot, grated
300 ml (½ pint) tomato juice
575 ml (1 pint) water
or vegetable stock (page 75)
5 ml (1 teaspoon) caraway seeds
salt, pepper and freshly grated nutmeg
150 ml carton of soured cream
or natural yoghurt, to serve

1 Put all the vegetables in large pan, with the tomato juice, stock or water and caraway seeds. Bring to the boil, cover and simmer for 45–60 minutes.
2 Season to taste with salt, pepper and nutmeg.
3 Serve as a coarsely textured soup or cool slightly and then liquidise until smooth.
4 Serve hot or cold, with a generous spoonful of cream or yoghurt floating on top.

SERVES 6
PREPARATION TIME:
10 minutes + 20 minutes cooking
FREEZING: recommended

15 ml (1 tablespoon) oil
1 onion, chopped
2 celery sticks, chopped
6 large tomatoes, quartered and de-seeded
2 bay leaves
850 ml (1½ pints) chicken stock (page 77)
15 ml (1 tablespoon) cornflour
grated zest and juice of 1 orange
salt, pepper and sugar
90 ml (6 tablespoons) cream, to serve

TOMATO & ORANGE SOUP

1 In a large pan, heat the oil and sauté the onion and celery for 3–4 minutes, until softened but not brown.
2 Add the tomatoes, bay leaves and stock.
3 Bring to the boil and simmer for 20 minutes or until the vegetables are tender.
4 Leave to cool for a moment. Remove the bay leaves. Purée the soup and then return to the pan.
5 Blend the cornflour with a little water and blend into the soup, stirring all the time until completely mixed in. Heat gently until slightly thickened.
6 Add the orange zest. Stir in the orange juice and season with salt, pepper and sugar to taste.
7 Divide between serving bowls and add a swirl of cream to each.

SERVES 4
PREPARATION TIME:
10 minutes + 15 minutes cooking
FREEZING: recommended

350 g (12 oz) carrots, sliced
575 ml (1 pint) vegetable stock (page 75)
a knob of fresh root ginger, crushed
40 g (1½ oz) butter
2 onions, sliced
5 ml (1 teaspoon) ground ginger
5 ml (1 teaspoon) grated orange zest
30 ml (2 tablespoons) orange juice
salt and freshly ground pepper
60 ml (4 tablespoons) whipping cream, whipped, to serve

CARROT & GINGER SOUP

1 Place the carrots, stock and ginger in a pan. Bring to the boil and simmer for 15 minutes. Discard the ginger.
2 Meanwhile, melt the butter in a saucepan; add the onion and fry gently until soft.
3 Stir in the ground ginger and orange zest and then add the cooked carrots and their cooking stock. Cover the pan, bring to the boil and simmer for 10 minutes.
4 Allow to cool slightly and then purée the soup. Return the purée to the pan, add the orange juice and season to taste with salt and pepper.
5 Reheat the soup. Serve in individual bowls with a spoonful of the whipped cream floating on top.

SERVES 4
PREPARATION TIME:
10 minutes + 15 minutes cooking
FREEZING: recommended

25 g (1 oz) butter
1 onion, chopped finely
1 potato, diced
½ head of celery, chopped, leaves reserved to garnish
80 g (3 oz) cashew nuts, chopped roughly
700 ml (1¼ pints) vegetable stock (page 75)
15 g (½ oz) plain flour
450 ml (16 fl oz) milk
salt and pepper

CELERY & CASHEW NUT SOUP

1 Gently melt the butter in a large saucepan.
2 Add the onion and potato and cook for 5 minutes.
3 Stir in the celery and nuts and cook for a further 5 minutes.
4 Stir in the stock, bring to the boil and then reduce the heat and simmer for 15 minutes.
5 Blend the flour with a little of the milk, stir in the remainder of the milk and pour into the soup, stirring until the soup has thickened. Gently reheat but do not allow to boil.
6 Adjust the seasoning and serve garnished with celery leaves, if you have any.

SERVES 4
PREPARATION & COOKING TIME: 40 minutes
FREEZING: not recommended

ASPARAGUS & PEA SOUP

This soup is almost as good made at any time of year with canned asparagus and frozen peas.

850 ml (1³/₄ pints) chicken stock (page 77)
450 g (1 lb) asparagus spears
225 g (8 oz) shelled fresh peas
1 fresh mint sprig
40 g (1¹/₂ oz) butter
40 g (1¹/₂ oz) plain flour
300 ml (¹/₂ pint) milk
salt and freshly ground black pepper
60 ml (4 tablespoons) cream, to serve

1 Into a large saucepan, put the stock, asparagus, peas and mint. Bring to the boil and simmer for 10–15 minutes, until tender.
2 Meanwhile, blend the butter and flour. Bring the milk to the boil and whisk walnut-sized pieces of the blended butter and flour into the milk. Continue cooking until the sauce has thickened.
3 Allow the soup to cool slightly and then purée it.
4 Mix the soup and sauce together. Reheat gently, without allowing it to boil. Adjust the seasoning.
5 Divide between individual bowls and serve each with a swirl of cream.

SERVES 4–6
PREPARATION TIME: 30 minutes + 30 minutes cooking
FREEZING: recommended, after step 3

LEEK & POTATO SOUP WITH LAVENDER

Flowers and herbs give soups a unique flavour; lavender has been used in cooking for many years but is an unusual ingredient to find in a soup because it is normally used for aroma rather than taste. It is fairly pungent, so do not exceed the quantity recommended.

15 ml (1 tablespoon) oil
2 leeks, chopped
450 g (1 lb) potatoes, chopped
1 litre (1³/₄ pints) vegetable stock (page 75)
300 ml (¹/₂ pint) milk
6 lavender flower heads, tied in a piece of muslin
salt and freshly ground black pepper
60–90 ml (4–6 tablespoons) crème fraîche, to serve

1 In a large saucepan, heat the oil and sauté the leeks until soft but not brown. Add the potatoes and stir thoroughly.
2 Add the stock, milk and lavender flowers. Bring to the boil, cover and simmer for about 30 minutes or until the vegetables are tender.
3 Allow to cool slightly, remove the bundle of lavender and then reduce to a purée. Return to the saucepan, adjust the seasoning and reheat gently.
4 Put a spoonful of crème fraîche on each bowlful, to serve.

SERVES 6
PREPARATION TIME: 20 minutes + 30 minutes cooking
FREEZING: recommended

GRANNY SMITH'S TOMATO & CARROT SOUP

15 g (½ oz) butter
45 ml (3 tablespoons) vegetable oil
2 onions, chopped finely
I fat garlic clove, chopped finely
350 g (12 oz) carrots, chopped
675 g (1½ lb) ripe, juicy tomatoes, skinned, de-seeded
    and chopped (see **Note**)
2 Granny Smith apples, peeled, cored and chopped small
1.7 litres (3 pints) vegetable or chicken stock (page 75 or 77)
a bouquet garni of I fresh thyme sprig, I fresh marjoram sprig
    and I bay leaf, or I teaspoon each dried thyme and marjoram
salt and pepper
chopped fresh parsley, to garnish

1   Using a large pan, melt the butter, add the oil and slowly fry the onion and the garlic until soft. This might take up to 10 minutes.
2   Add the carrots to the pan and stir round and cook for a further 5 minutes. Now add the tomatoes, apples, stock and herbs.
3   Bring to the boil and then reduce the heat and leave to simmer for about 30 minutes. Stir often and leave the lid on but tilted to one side.
4   Remove the herbs and leave to cool slightly. Then reduce the soup to a purée. Season with salt and pepper. Serve hot with a sprinkling of parsley.

NOTE: To skin tomatoes, put them in a bowl and pour boiling water over them to cover. Leave for a minute or two and then make a small slit in one end and slip the skins off.

SERVES 4
PREPARATION TIME: 25 minutes + 45 minutes cooking
FREEZING: recommended

ROASTED RED PEPPER & TOMATO SOUP

An interesting soup with a lovely colour and flavour; it can be served either hot or cold.

4 red peppers, cut in half lengthways and de-seeded
6 ripe tomatoes, skinned (see note opposite) and halved
15 ml (I tablespoon) oil
5 ml (I teaspoon) sugar
15 ml (I tablespoon) chopped fresh basil
I onion, chopped finely
I garlic clove, chopped finely or crushed
575 ml (I pint) vegetable stock (page 75)
salt and freshly ground black pepper
chopped fresh basil, to garnish.

1   Preheat the oven to 190°C/170°C fan oven/Gas Mark 5.
2   Place the peppers, skin-side up, and the tomatoes, cut-side up, on a baking tray. Drizzle with half the oil and sprinkle with the sugar and chopped basil. Roast in the oven for 30 minutes.
3   Meanwhile, in a large saucepan, sauté the onion and garlic in the remaining oil until soft but not browned.
4   Remove the skins from the peppers. Add the peppers, tomatoes and any juices to the saucepan, cover with the stock, and bring to the boil. Turn down the heat and simmer for 15 minutes.
5   Cool slightly and then liquidise until smooth.
6   Season to taste with salt and pepper and gently reheat. Serve garnished with chopped basil.

SERVES 4
PREPARATION TIME:
35 minutes + 30 minutes cooking
FREEZING: recommended

Grace's good friend Nona hates onion and this is her recipe for a very nice soup with carrots and courgettes.

50 g (2 oz) butter
450 g (1 lb) firm, shiny courgettes, sliced
450 g (1 lb) fresh, hard carrots, sliced
850 ml (1½ pints) chicken stock (page 77)
4 small bay leaves
salt and pepper
60 ml (4 tablespoons) double cream,
    to serve (optional)

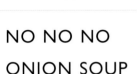

NO NO NO
ONION SOUP

1 Melt the butter in a roomy pan. Add the courgettes and carrots and sweat for about 5–6 minutes over a high heat, covered, shaking the pan from time to time, without allowing them to brown.
2 Pour in just 575 ml (1 pint) of the stock, reserving the rest for later. Add the bay leaves and bring back to the boil. Reduce the heat and leave to simmer for 20–30 minutes or until the vegetables are soft.
3 Remove the bay leaves, leave to cool a little and then use a hand-blender to reduce the soup to a smooth consistency.
4 Add the remaining stock and season to taste with salt and pepper.
5 Reheat and serve with cream, if using, swirled into each serving.

SERVES 4
PREPARATION & COOKING TIME: 30 minutes
FREEZING: recommended

Grace says: 'This was the first cold soup I ever tasted. It was in Spain, and I've enjoyed it ever since. My early attempts to imitate it were rather drab, until I got some tomatoes which had had the benefit of the sun. Outdoor tomatoes that are very ripe are the best choice for this soup; next-best are vine tomatoes or plum tomatoes'.

GAZPACHO

90 ml (6 tablespoons) good-quality
    extra-virgin olive oil
15 ml (1 tablespoon) finely chopped onion
2 fat garlic cloves, chopped finely
    and then crushed
2 red peppers, chopped roughly
1 yellow pepper, chopped roughly
7–8 very ripe tomatoes, chopped roughly
½ large cucumber, chopped roughly,
    or a sweetly-flavoured small cucumber
575 ml (1 pint) chicken stock (page 77)
2 fat pinches of caster sugar
10 ml (2 teaspoons) tomato purée
Tabasco or chilli sauce
white-wine vinegar
a large handful of fresh herbs,
    e.g. basil, tarragon and chervil
snipped fresh chives, to garnish

1 Heat a tablespoon of the oil in a pan and gently fry the onion and garlic. Keep the lid on and shake the pan often to soften the onions. Set this pan aside to go cold.
2 Set aside a small piece each of red pepper and yellow pepper. Put the rest of the peppers, the tomatoes, and cucumber into a food processor or blender, with the remaining oil, chicken stock, sugar, tomato purée, 1–2 shakes of Tabasco sauce, a dash of white-wine vinegar, the cooked onion and garlic and the herbs.
3 Whiz to a smoothish purée. Pour through a nylon sieve.
4 Store in a fridge until needed.
5 Serve in small bowls, with a few bits of reserved and chopped red and yellow pepper and chives scattered over.

SERVES 4
PREPARATION & COOKING TIME:
20 minutes
FREEZING: recommended

This clear soup full of vegetables and noodles is typically Chinese. The pak choi heads, now available in the bigger supermarkets, look like a thinner green version of a head of celery. Grace tends to use most of the greenery from the top of the head in a salad or stir-fry and concentrates on the vivid green stalks for the soup. Thread noodles are the fine ones, which you just soak in boiling water and they are ready to eat. The brown mushrooms used in this recipe are ideal because, when cooked, they stay fairly firm and have a good flavour.

1 litre (1³/₄ pints) well flavoured chicken stock (page 77)
5 ml (1 teaspoon) finely chopped fresh root ginger
1 small red chilli, de-seeded and chopped finely
juice of ¹/₂ lime (about 15ml/1 tablespoon)
15 ml (1 tablespoon) light soy sauce
50 g (2 oz) brown mushrooms (sometimes called Paris or chestnut mushrooms)
2 pak choi heads, finely sliced
150 g (5 oz) fine thread egg noodles
30 ml (2 tablespoons) chopped fresh coriander

1 Put the chicken stock, ginger, chilli, lime juice and light soy sauce in a roomy pan. Over a moderate heat, simmer for 5 minutes.
2 Stir in the mushrooms and the pak choi and continue cooking for another 5–7 minutes or until the green stems are cooked but not soggy.
3 Place the noodles in a bowl and pour boiling water over them. Stir to separate the strands and then drain off the water and divide the wet noodles between four warm bowls.
4 Top up with the soup and decorate each bowl with chopped coriander.

CHINESE PAK CHOI & NOODLE SOUP

SERVES 4–5
PREPARATION TIME: 10 minutes + 20 minutes cooking
FREEZING: recommended

SERVES 4
PREPARATION TIME: 5–20 minutes (depending on whether you have to shell the beans and peas) + 15 minutes cooking
FREEZING: recommended

LEEK & FENNEL SOUP

BROAD BEAN SOUP

This soup has a delicate flavour and will make a delicious starter to any meal. Fennel and leeks are both available all year round. Use only the whites of the leeks and well rounded fennel.

Broad beans are Dilwen's favourite vegetable. Provided they're eaten young they have a delicate flavour. They freeze well and are delicious with ham or bacon, hence this soup.

15 ml (1 tablespoon) oil
25 g (1 oz) butter
900 g (2 lb) leeks, white only, sliced
1 large fennel bulb, trimmed and sliced, leaves reserved to garnish
1 garlic clove, crushed
30 ml (2 tablespoons) plain flour
850 ml (1½ pints) vegetable or chicken stock (page 75 or 77)
salt and pepper

25 g (1 oz) butter
1 onion, chopped
225 g (8 oz) podded and shelled fresh, or frozen, broad beans
175 g (6 oz) shelled fresh, or frozen, peas
425 ml (¾ pint) vegetable stock (page 75)
115 g (4 oz) good-quality ham, cubed, or lean cooked bacon, chopped
425 ml (¾ pint) milk
salt and freshly ground pepper

1   Heat the oil and butter in a large saucepan, add the leeks, fennel and garlic and sauté for 5 minutes, stirring occasionally. Do not allow to brown.
2   Add the flour and stir well. Pour in the stock and make sure the flour is well blended. Then bring to the boil, cover and simmer for 20 minutes.
3   Leave to a cool for a short time. Purée until smooth.
4   Return to the pan and season to taste. Reheat gently.
5   Serve garnished with the chopped fennel leaves.

1   Heat the butter in a large pan and then sauté the onion until softened.
2   Add the beans and peas and the stock, with half the ham or bacon and bring to the boil. Reduce the heat and simmer for 15 minutes, or until the vegetables are tender.
3   Leave to cool slightly and then purée half the soup.
4   Return the soup to the pan, add the milk and mix well. Adjust the seasoning and reheat.
5   Serve garnished with the remaining ham or bacon.

SERVES 6
PREPARATION TIME:
10 minutes + 15 minutes cooking + 2 hours chilling
FREEZING: recommended

SERVES 4
PREPARATION & COOKING TIME: 40 minutes
FREEZING: recommended

SORREL & CUCUMBER SOUP

FISH SOUP

Sorrel is not used a lot in home cooking but it is well worth a try. It has a sharp, lemony taste and used to be very popular in a sauce for poached salmon. Sorrel grows wild in some areas but Grace gets hers in generous bunches from York Market. The leaves are about the size of a beech leaf and are easy to deal with because of that.

I generous bunch of sorrel leaves, rinsed and picked over, torn up, stems discarded
I thin fresh cucumber, chopped (the fat ones have rather big seeds)
1.1 litres (2 pints) chicken stock (page 77)
3 fat spring onions, chopped
I garlic clove, sliced
150 ml carton of single cream
salt and pepper

I Simmer the sorrel, cucumber, stock, spring onions and garlic together in a pan until the cucumber and spring onions are soft.
2 Allow this to cool and then reduce the soup to a purée.
3 Pour in the single cream, stir in well and season to taste with salt and pepper. Chill for at least an hour or until ready to serve.
4 Serve cold, in small bowls.

This is a low-fat soup but piquant and satisfying. If the taste is too sharp, add a little sugar.

2 onions, sliced
I leek, white part only, sliced
3 fat garlic cloves, crushed
700 ml (1 1/4 pints) fish stock (page 75)
I red pepper, de-seeded and chopped
450 g (1 lb) fresh tomatoes, skinned and chopped
15 ml (1 tablespoon) tomato purée
juice of I lemon and grated zest of 1/2 lemon
I small cooking apple, cored and chopped
45 ml (3 tablespoons) dry white wine
a bouquet garni of I fresh thyme sprig, I fresh marjoram sprig and 3 fresh parsley sprigs, tied with string or white cotton
450 g (1 lb) white fish, cut into bite-sized pieces
45 ml (3 tablespoons) chopped fresh parsley
salt and freshly ground black pepper

I Soften the onion, leek and garlic in a little of the stock in a large pan over a medium heat for 10 minutes.
2 Add the stock, pepper, tomatoes, tomato purée, lemon zest and juice, apple and wine. Drop in the bouquet garni.
3 Bring to the boil, reduce the heat and simmer for 10 minutes.
4 Remove the bouquet garni. Add the fish and gently simmer for 5 minutes.
5 Adjust the seasoning and stir in most of the parsley.
6 Serve with the remaining parsley scattered on top.

LAMB & LEEK SOUP *pictured opposite*

SERVES 4
PREPARATION & COOKING TIME:
I hour
FREEZING: recommended

25 g (I oz) butter
225 g (6 oz) neck fillet of lamb, cubed
I large onion, chopped
450 g (I lb) mixed root vegetables,
e.g. carrots, swede and parsnip, chopped
1.1 litres (2 pints) chicken stock (page 77)
I potato, chopped
225 g (8 oz) leeks, sliced
juice of ¹/₂ lemon
30 ml (2 tablespoons) chopped fresh parsley
salt and pepper

This is a modern version of Scotch broth or Welsh cawl.

1 In a large pan, melt the butter and sauté the lamb cubes until slightly brown. Remove from the pan.
2 Soften the onion in the same pan for 5 minutes,
3 Return the lamb to the pan, with the root vegetables. Add the stock, bring to the boil and simmer for 15 minutes.
4 Add the potato. Simmer for a further 10 minutes
5 Add the leeks and simmer for a further 5–10 minutes
6 Adjust the seasoning and add lemon juice to taste. Add the parsley, reserving a little to sprinkle on top, and serve at once.

COURGETTE & MINT SOUP

SERVES 4
PREPARATION TIME:
30 minutes + 20 minutes cooking
FREEZING: recommended after step 3

25 g (I oz) butter
I onion, chopped
450 g (I lb) courgettes, chopped into chunks
700 ml (1¹/₄ pints) chicken
or vegetable stock (page 75 or 77)
a handful of fresh mint leaves
salt and pepper
60 ml (4 tablespoons) natural yoghurt,
to serve
4 small fresh mint sprigs or leaves,
to garnish

1 Melt the butter in a large pan and cook the onion for 5 minutes over a gentle heat, until soft and transparent. Add the courgettes and cook for a further 5 minutes.
2 Add the stock and half the mint leaves. Cover the pan, bring to the boil and simmer for 20 minutes. Cool slightly
3 Add the remaining mint leaves and purée the soup. (Adding the mint in two batches preserves the flavour of the fresh herb in the finished soup.) Season to taste with salt and pepper.
4 If serving hot, reheat gently.
5 To serve cold, chill the soup for several hours.
6 Serve with a swirl of yoghurt and a few mint leaves to garnish.

SERVES 4–6
PREPARATION & COOKING TIME: 40 minutes
FREEZING: recommended

GREEN PEA & CABBAGE SOUP

Grace says: 'I live in an area where peas are grown in quantity. A generous neighbour often brings me a bucketfull straight from the field! I blanch and freeze the peas and keep an eye open for good recipes in which to use them. This recipe was originally written by Linda Tubby – here is my version, in which the two vegetables are cooked separately and then amalgamated at the end'.

150 g (5 oz) butter
350 g (12 oz) fresh shelled or frozen peas
425 ml (15 fl oz) water
675 g (1 lb 8 oz) spring greens or savoy cabbage (not the hard white
  variety), chopped finely and coarse stems discarded
575 ml (1 pint) vegetable or chicken stock (page 75 or 77)
5 ml (1 teaspoon) white sugar
10 ml (2 teaspoons) salt
freshly ground black pepper

1   Melt 50 g (2 oz) of the butter in a pan and stir in the peas plus 150 ml (¼ pint) of the water. Simmer for 2–3 minutes or until the peas are cooked.
2   Remove the pan from the heat, allow to cool slightly and then reduce the peas to a purée.
3   Empty the pea mixture into a bowl and wash the pan. Melt the rest of the butter and stir in the cabbage. Cook gently until the cabbage is starting to soften.
4   Stir in the stock, remaining water, sugar and salt. Simmer until the cabbage is well cooked – about 5–10 minutes.
5   Use the hand-blender again to reduce the cabbage almost to a purée. I like to see bits of green in the soup.
6   Stir the pea purée into the cabbage. Reheat and serve with a rough grinding of pepper on each serving.

SERVES 6
PREPARATION & COOKING TIME: 40 minutes
FREEZING: recommended

GREEN VEGETABLE SOUP

Not only does this soup taste delicious but it uses up broccoli stems, the parts you normally discard – though they are actually full of flavour – and asparagus stalks. So, if you are using just the tips of asparagus, for example in a pasta dish or to serve with grilled sole or plaice, this soup is good way to use up the leftover stems.

50 g (2 oz) butter
225 g (8 oz) asparagus stalks
450 g (1 lb) broccoli, stems only
1 leek, sliced
4 spring onions, chopped.
225 g (8 oz) shelled fresh, or frozen, peas
175 g (6 oz) french or green beans
1.1 litres (2 pints) vegetable stock (page 75)
1 fresh parsley sprig
1 fresh thyme sprig
salt and pepper

1   Melt the butter in a large pan. Put the asparagus stalks and the remaining vegetables in the pan. Cover and sweat for approximately 10 minutes.
3   Add the stock and herbs, bring to the boil and simmer for 10–15 minutes until the vegetables are tender. Remove the thyme sprig.
4   Allow to cool slightly and then liquidise until smooth. Return to the pan, check the seasoning and gently reheat before serving.

SERVES 4–5
PREPARATION TIME: 35 minutes + 30 minutes cooking
FREEZING: recommended

FRESH TOMATO & BASIL SOUP

Basil and tomatoes are a perfect flavour combination and the shallots give the soup a slight sweetness.

50 g (2 oz) butter or 30 ml (2 tablespoons) oil
6 shallots, chopped
I garlic clove, crushed or chopped
30 ml (2 tablespoons) plain flour
850 ml (1½ pints) chicken stock (page 77)
900 g (2 lb) beef tomatoes, skinned (page 30) and chopped roughly
30 ml (2 tablespoons) tomato purée
45 ml (3 tablespoons) chopped fresh basil
salt and freshly ground black pepper
chopped fresh basil, to garnish

1 Heat the butter or oil in a large saucepan and cook the shallots and garlic for 3 minutes, stirring occasionally.
2 Add the flour and cook for I minute, stirring all the time.
3 Gradually add the stock and bring to the boil, stirring all the time until thickened.
4 Stir in the tomatoes, tomato purée and fresh basil, season well; cover and simmer for 30 minutes.
5 Cool slightly and then purée until smooth. Reheat and serve garnished with more chopped basil.

SERVES 4–5
PREPARATION & COOKING TIME: 45 minutes
FREEZING: not recommended

TARRAGON CHICKEN SOUP

25 g (I oz) butter
I large onion, sliced finely
30 ml (2 tablespoons) plain flour
850 ml (1½ pints) chicken stock (page 77)
finely grated zest and juice of ½ lemon
225 g (8 oz) cooked chicken,
    skinned and cubed
15 ml (I tablespoon) chopped fresh tarragon
150 ml carton of double cream
salt and freshly ground white pepper
slices of lemon and fresh tarragon sprigs,
    to garnish

1 Heat the butter in a large saucepan and sauté the onion for 5 minutes, without browning, stirring occasionally.
2 Add the flour and cook for I minute, stirring all the time.
3 Gradually add the stock, making sure all the flour is well blended, and bring to the boil, stirring until thickened.
4 Add the lemon zest and juice, cover and simmer for 10 minutes.
5 Add the chicken and tarragon and simmer for a further 5 minutes.
6 Remove the soup from the heat and stir in the cream. Season to taste with salt and white pepper.
7 Reheat gently but do not allow to boil. Serve garnished with lemon slices and sprigs of fresh tarragon.

Grace says: **'I fall with joy on any recipe which uses lovage, which grows like a weed in my garden and seeds everywhere.** The maddening thing is that the flavour of the leaves is so powerful you rarely need more than three of them; even this recipe needs only 25 g (1 oz). I advise you to pick the young top leaves as the lower ones get very tough. By the way, I must also warn you that lovage grows very quickly into a tall bush!'

SERVES 6
PREPARATION TIME:
20 minutes + 20 minutes cooking
FREEZING: recommended

LETTUCE & LOVAGE SOUP

'This recipe is based on the excellent book of soups by New Covent Garden Soup Company, though I have altered the recipe slightly. They describe lovage as having an intense, celery-like flavour and say it was once called sea parsley. My thanks to the company for a great recipe, which also uses up that flush of lettuce which comes to all of us in summer. You'll get rid of 1.5 kg (3 lb 5 oz)! (I used Webb's Wonder and it was excellent but cos or little gem would work well too.)'

25 g (1 oz) butter
175 g (6 oz) spring onions, chopped
250 g (9 oz) potatoes, chopped small
1.5 kg (3 lb 5 oz) iceberg
   or any crisp lettuce, chopped
575 ml (1 pint) vegetable stock (page 77)
30 ml (2 tablespoons) lemon juice
25 g (1 oz) young lovage leaves,
   hard stems removed, chopped
425 ml (15 fl oz) milk
300 ml carton of single cream
salt and white pepper
tiny lovage leaves, to garnish

1   In a roomy pan, melt the butter and gently cook the spring onions, covered, and without burning, until soft. Add the potatoes, lettuce, vegetable stock and lemon juice and cover again.
2   Bring to the boil and then reduce the heat and simmer gently for about 15 minutes, until the vegetables are tender.
3   Cool a little and then reduce to a purée. Return the soup to a clean pan.
4   Stir in the lovage and simmer gently, covered, for a further 5 minutes.
5   Stir in the milk and cream, and season to taste with salt and white pepper.
6   Reheat gently and serve with one or two baby lovage leaves floating on each serving.

AUTUMN SOUPS

SERVES 4–6
PREPARATION TIME:
30 minutes + 20 minutes cooking
FREEZING:
recommended, without the sausage slices

15 ml (1 tablespoon) oil
1 large onion, chopped
2 carrots, diced
425 g can of kidney beans, drained
5 ml (1 teaspoon) chilli powder
225 g can of chopped tomatoes
15 ml (1 tablespoon) tomato purée
850 ml (1½ pints) chicken stock (page 77)
salt and freshly ground black pepper
sliced spicy sausage, to serve

CHILLI
BEAN SOUP

1 Heat the oil in a large saucepan. Add the onion and carrot and sauté over a medium heat until the vegetables are soft but not browned. Stir occasionally.
2 Add the kidney beans and chilli powder. Cook for 1 minute.
3 Add the tomatoes, tomato purée, stock and seasoning. Bring to the boil, reduce the heat, cover and simmer for 20 minutes.
4 Allow to cool slightly and then purée half the soup until coarsely chopped.
5 Return to the remaining soup in the pan and reheat.
6 Serve each portion with a few small slices of spicy sausage.

SERVES 6
PREPARATION TIME: 35 minutes + 30 minutes marinating + 1 hour cooking
FREEZING: recommended

Roasting the vegetables for the soup is well worth the effort. It gives the soup a very different flavour from a soup made with the same raw vegetables. Vary the vegetables according to your taste and what is available.

This recipe was sent in by Sîan Cook, author of the WI Book of Vegetarian Cuisine and Best-Kept Secrets of the WI: Puddings and Desserts. It is now one of Dilwen's family's favourite soups and when she is roasting vegetables for a meal she always does extra vegetables to make this soup.

ROASTED ROOT
VEGETABLE SOUP

450 g (1lb) celeriac, cut into wedges
1 large parsnip, quartered lengthways
2 carrots, halved lengthways
8 shallots
1 large sweet potato, cut into 8
45 ml (3 tablespoons) olive oil
15 ml (1 tablespoon) chopped fresh parsley
15 ml (1 tablespoon) fresh thyme leaves
850 ml (1½ pints) vegetable stock (page 75)
salt and freshly ground pepper
90 ml (6 tablespoons) single cream
    or natural yoghurt, to serve

1 Toss the vegetables in the oil and sprinkle with the herbs and salt and pepper. Marinate for at least half an hour.
2 Preheat the oven to 220°C/440°F/Gas Mark 8. Roast the vegetables for 45 minutes, until the vegetables are beginning to brown.
3 Transfer to a large saucepan. Add the stock, bring to the boil and simmer for 15 minutes or until the vegetables are tender.
4 Liquidise the soup. Return to the pan and gently reheat. Check the seasoning.
5 Transfer to six bowls and serve each with a swirl of cream or yoghurt.

SERVES 4

PREPARATION TIME:

10 minutes + 40 minutes cooking

FREEZING: recommended after step 3

25 g (1 oz) butter

1 onion, chopped

225 g (8 oz) potato, chopped

450 g (1 lb) cooked beetroot, sliced

575 ml (1 pint) vegetable stock (page 75)

300 ml (1/2 pint) milk

10 ml (2 teaspoons) ground cumin

juice and grated zest of 1 lemon

150 ml (5 fl oz) double cream
   or natural yoghurt

salt and pepper

snipped fresh chives, to garnish

BEETROOT SOUP

1 Melt the butter in a roomy pan and sauté the onion until soft. Then stir in the potato and sweat for 3–4 minutes, covered, shaking the pan occasionally.
2 Stir in the beetroot, vegetable stock and milk, bring to the boil and simmer for 15 minutes.
3 Add the cumin and lemon zest and juice.
4 Allow to cool a little and then reduce to a purée.
5 Season to taste, stir in the cream or yoghurt and carefully reheat. Be careful not to let the soup boil after this point or it will curdle.
6 Garnish with fresh chives and serve immediately.

SERVES 4

PREPARATION TIME:

15 minutes + 20 minutes cooking

FREEZING: recommended

30 ml (2 tablespoons) olive oil

1 large onion, chopped

2 garlic cloves, crushed

450 g (1 lb) courgettes, sliced

225 g (8 oz) potato, chopped

5 ml (1 teaspoon) chopped fresh parsley

700 ml (1 1/4 pints) vegetable stock (page 75)

80 g (3 oz) feta cheese

salt and pepper

chopped fresh parsley, to garnish

COURGETTE & FETA SOUP

1 In a large pan, heat the oil and soften the onion and garlic.
2 Add the courgette and potato and sauté for about 10 minutes.
3 Add the parsley and stock, bring to the boil and cook for 15–20 minutes or until the vegetables are softened.
4 Allow the soup to cool slightly and then reduce to a purée.
5 Add the feta cheese and, off the heat, stir until melted.
6 Gently reheat the soup, without allowing it to boil. Check the seasoning and serve with a scattering of parsley on top.

SERVES 6

PREPARATION & COOKING TIME:

45 minutes

FREEZING: recommended

1 large onion, chopped

1 carrot, chopped

1 yellow pepper, de-seeded and chopped

350 g (12 oz) sweet potato, cubed

400 g (14 oz) fresh, defrosted frozen,
   or drained canned sweetcorn kernels

1.3 litre (2 1/4 pints) vegetable stock (page 75)

80 g (3 oz) small pasta shells

salt and pepper

chopped fresh parsley, to garnish

GOLDEN VEGETABLE SOUP WITH PASTA

1 Into a large pan, put all the vegetables and the stock.
2 Bring to the boil and then reduce the heat and simmer for 15 minutes.
3 Add the pasta and simmer until both the vegetables and the pasta are tender.
4 Adjust the seasoning.
5 Serve garnished with chopped parsley.

SERVES 4
PREPARATION & COOKING TIME:
1 hour
FREEZING: not recommended

For a real treat on a special occasion, Dilwen, who loves mussels, makes a mussel soup. It is a complete meal in itself. Mussels are plentiful around Caernarfon and Bangor in North Wales and they are reputed to be some of the finest harvested in this country.

2 kg (4¹/₂ lb) fresh mussels
300 ml (¹/₂ pint) dry white wine
2 bay leaves
6 black peppercorns
25 g (1 oz) butter
1 large onion, chopped
4 garlic cloves, crushed
300 ml (¹/₂ pint) milk
150 ml carton of cream
30 ml (2 tablespoons) chopped fresh parsley
salt and pepper

1   Wash the mussels several times to remove any sand. Remove the 'beards' and discard any mussels that are not closed

2   Put the wine in a large saucepan, with the bay leaves and the peppercorns, and bring to the boil. Add the mussels, cover with a tightly fitting lid and cook on a high heat for 3–4 minutes, shaking the pan to ensure they all cook.

3   Discard any mussels that have not opened. Drain and reserve the liquor and remove the mussels from their shells.

4   Melt the butter in the pan and soften the onion and garlic.

5   Add the strained mussel liquor and the milk. Bring to the boil and then reduce the heat and leave to simmer until the onions and garlic are cooked

6   Adjust the seasoning. Add the mussels, cream and parsley. Reheat gently, without boiling and serve immediately.

MUSSEL SOUP

SERVES 4
PREPARATION TIME:
12 hours soaking + 20 minutes + 1³/₄ hours cooking
FREEZING: recommended

BUTTER-BEAN & CELERIAC SOUP

225 g (8 oz) dried butter-beans, soaked for 12 hours
1 litre (1³/₄ pints) vegetable stock (page 75)
2 onions, chopped
1 celeriac, peeled and chopped
5 ml (1 teaspoon) caraway seeds
30 ml (2 tablespoons) chopped fresh parsley
575 ml (1 pint) milk
salt and pepper

1 Drain the beans, rinse well, and transfer to a large pan. Pour in the stock, bring to the boil and cook for 1 hour.
2 Add the onion, celeriac, caraway seeds and parsley and simmer until the beans are tender (about another 45 minutes).
3 Allow to cool a little and then purée the soup. Add the milk, adjust the seasoning, and reheat gently, without boiling, before serving.

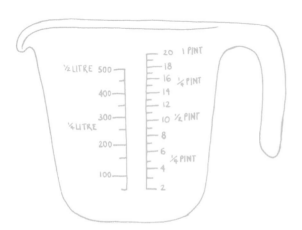

SERVES 5–6
PREPARATION & COOKING TIME: 45 minutes
FREEZING: recommended, after step 6

MUSHROOM SOUP THICKENED WITH TOAST

This soup is thickened with toast, as an alternative to flour or egg.

2 thick slices of white bread, crusts removed
50 g (2 oz) butter
400 g (14 oz) chestnut (Paris) mushrooms, chopped, or ordinary mushrooms if these are not available
1 fat garlic clove
450 ml (16 fl oz) double cream
150 ml (¹/₄ pint) vegetable or chicken stock (page 75 or 77)
salt and freshly ground pepper
oil, for frying

1 Toast the bread thoroughly. When it is cold and dry, put it in the food processor and reduce it to a fine powder.
2 Melt the butter in a roomy pan. Set aside four small mushrooms and add the remaining mushrooms to the pan. Grate the clove of garlic straight into the pan, using the coarse side of a metal grater.
3 Cook the mushrooms and garlic until soft. If the mushrooms stick, add a dash of water, stirring often.
4 Add the cream and stock to the pan and continue to simmer for about 10 minutes.
5 While this is cooking, slice the reserved mushrooms downwards into four slices and fry in oil until they are soft. Set aside and keep warm.
6 Allow the soup to cool briefly and then blend the soup until smooth. Season to taste and then stir in enough of the powdered toast to give the consistency you like.
7 Serve piping hot, topping each bowlful with a couple of slices of fried mushrooms.

SERVES 7–8
PREPARATION TIME: 45 minutes + 45 minutes cooking
FREEZING: recommended

PUMPKIN & APPLE SOUP WITH MINT

Grace brought this recipe back from Australia, where pumpkins are used a lot for soup and also for roasting in large chunks. One of the most popular pumpkins is not the familiar round shape but like a giant peanut in its shell. It is about the size of a melon with a waist. This recipe works with any kind of pumpkin and the soup is a lovely orange colour.

80 g (3 oz) butter
2 large onions, sliced
1 kg (2 lb 2 oz) peeled and de-seeded pumpkin flesh, chopped
1 large carrot, chopped
1 large ripe tomato, chopped
1 Granny Smith apple, peeled, cored and chopped
2.5 ml (1/2 teaspoon) salt
2.5 ml (1/2 teaspoon) curry powder
1.1 litres (2 pints) water
pepper
45 ml (3 tablespoons) chopped fresh mint, to garnish

1 In a very large pan, melt the butter and sweat the onion for at least 10 minutes. This is best done with the lid on but you must keep shaking and stirring as well.
2 Add everything else except the mint. Stir well. Bring to the boil and then reduce the heat and leave to a simmer for about 45 minutes or until all the vegetables are soft.
3 Remove the pan from the heat, leave to cool for a little and then reduce the contents to a purée, which you will have to do in batches.
4 If the purée is too thick, add a little more water. Taste and adjust the seasoning.
5 Serve hot and scatter the mint generously over the surface of each serving.

SERVES 4
PREPARATION TIME: 30 minutes + 45 minutes cooking
FREEZING: recommended

CURRIED PARSNIP SOUP

30 ml (1 tablespoon) oil
450 g (1 lb) parsnips, sliced
1 onion, chopped
5 ml (1 teaspoon) curry powder
700 ml (1 1/4 pints) vegetable stock (page 75)
150 ml (1/4 pint) milk
salt and pepper
chopped fresh parsley, to garnish

1 In a large pan, heat the oil and fry the parsnip and onion for 10 minutes, without letting them brown.
2 Add the curry powder and cook for 2–3 minutes. Add the stock, milk and seasoning and simmer for 45 minutes.
3 Allow to cool slightly and then reduce to a purée.
4 Return to the clean pan and reheat gently. Serve piping-hot, sprinkled with parsley.

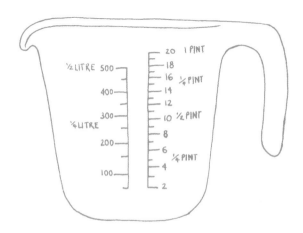

SERVES 4–5
PREPARATION TIME:
45 minutes + 25 minutes cooking
FREEZING:
recommended, without hazelnuts

This soup is made with the knobbly jerusalem artichokes. Grace has friends who cannot get rid of them from their garden and so she often finds a carrier bag of them hanging on her door handle! **Don't miss out the hazelnuts** – they are perfect with the soup.

40 g (1½ oz) butter
1 small onion, sliced finely
350 g (12 oz) jerusalem artichokes, scrubbed and sliced finely
575 ml (1 pint) chicken stock (page 77)
175 g (6 oz) young spinach leaves
300 ml (½ pint) milk
80 g (3 oz) whole skinned hazelnuts, toasted, if wished, and slivered (see Note)
salt, pepper and freshly grated nutmeg

1 Take a roomy pan and melt the butter. Fry the onion very gently until transparent and soft but not brown.
2 Stir in the artichokes. Continue to sweat the vegetables, covered, and shaking the pan well from time to time, for about 10 minutes.
3 Pour in the stock and add pepper and salt plus some freshly grated nutmeg to taste. (Grace would use half a whole nutmeg but use less if you wish.) Bring to the boil and then reduce the heat and simmer gently, stirring often, for about 20–25 minutes or until the artichokes are really soft.
4 Now rinse the spinach leaves and discard the tough stems and any slightly yellow leaves. Add the spinach to the soup and remove the pan from the hob. The spinach cooks enough in the residual heat of the pan and retains its colour.
5 Allow to cool a little and then reduce the soup to a purée. Stir in the milk and then gently reheat, without boiling. Serve hot, with the slivered hazelnuts sprinkled on top.

NOTE: The best way to sliver the hazelnuts is with the slicing disc on your food processor.

ARTICHOKE & SPINACH SOUP WITH HAZELNUTS

SERVES 4
PREPARATION & COOKING TIME: 20 minutes
FREEZING: recommended

SWEET POTATO & ORANGE SOUP

This soup is refreshing, slightly sweet and a delightful colour; it's the ideal remedy for jaded appetites. The soup can be cooked in the microwave.

25 g (I oz) butter
I onion, chopped
450 g (I lb) sweet potatoes, peeled and grated
2 celery sticks, very finely chopped
850 ml (I¹/₂ pints) vegetable stock (page 75)
2 fresh thyme sprigs
grated zest and juice of I orange
15 ml (I tablespoon) chopped fresh parsley
salt and pepper

1 Melt the butter in a large pan and then soften the onion, without browning
2 Add the sweet potatoes, celery, stock, thyme and orange zest. Bring to the boil and simmer for 10 minutes.
3 Remove the thyme and stir in the orange juice and parsley. Reheat gently, check the seasoning and serve immediately.

SERVES 4
PREPARATION TIME: 10 minutes + 30 minutes cooking
FREEZING: recommended

JERUSALEM ARTICHOKE & CARROT SOUP

This soup is nearly saffron coloured, due to the inclusion of carrots. It looks and tastes delicious and few people can guess what's in it. The artichokes discolour quickly so, as you peel each one, put it in a bowl of cold, salted water to keep the pale colour.

25 g (I oz) butter
I onion, chopped
2 celery sticks
I litre (I³/₄ pints) vegetable stock (page 75)
350 g (12 oz) jerusalem artichokes, peeled or scrubbed and chopped
225 g (8 oz) carrots, chopped
salt and pepper

1 In a large pan, melt the butter and then soften the onion and the celery for 5 minutes.
2 Add the stock and simmer for 20 minutes.
3 Add the artichokes and carrots and cook for a further 10 minutes.
4 Allow to cool slightly. Liquidise the soup until smooth. Return to the pan and reheat.
5 Adjust the seasoning and serve at once.

SERVES 4
PREPARATION & COOKING TIME: 1 hour
FREEZING: recommended

STILTON & PEAR SOUP

This delicious recipe was given to Grace by a farmer's wife, Liz Pexton. Her husband is a driving force in the NFU. Their farm is near Driffield in East Yorkshire and, along with a group of journalists, Grace was treated to a perfect lunch of soup and sandwiches when she went there as part of a group of writers visiting the East Riding to see and learn about pigs and cereals.

15 g (¹/₂ oz) butter
1 onion, finely chopped
4 ripe pears, peeled, cored and chopped
850 ml (1¹/₂ pints) chicken stock (page 77)
115 g (4 oz) Stilton cheese, crumbled
juice of ¹/₂ lemon (about 1¹/₂ tablespoons)
salt and freshly ground pepper
snipped fresh chives, to garnish

1 Melt the butter in a roomy pan and cook the onion slowly. Do not let it brown.
2 Add the pears, stock and seasoning. Simmer until the pears are tender (simmering time will depend on the type and ripeness of the pears).
3 Remove the pan from the heat and leave to cool for a little. Then purée the soup until it is smooth. Return the pan to the heat and reheat gently.
4 Add the crumbled Stilton and stir until it melts. Add the lemon juice to taste and adjust the seasoning.
5 Serve hot, with some snipped chives on each bowl.

SERVES 4
PREPARATION TIME: 45 minutes + 45 minutes cooking
FREEZING: recommended

SPLIT PEA & HAM SOUP

An old favourite, enhanced by the addition of a little nutmeg.

15 ml (1 tablespoon) oil
1 large onion, chopped
1 garlic clove, crushed or chopped
1.25 ml (¹/₄ teaspoon) freshly grated nutmeg
175 g (6 oz) gammon, chopped small
175 g (6 oz) dried split peas
850 ml (1¹/₂ pints) vegetable or chicken stock (page 75 or 77)
2.5 ml (¹/₂ teaspoon) sugar
150 ml carton of single cream
salt and freshly ground black pepper
chopped fresh parsley, to garnish

1 Heat the oil in a large saucepan, add the onion and garlic and sauté for 5 minutes, stirring occasionally. Add the nutmeg and gammon and cook for a further 5 minutes.
2 Add the peas and stock. Bring to the boil, cover and simmer for 45 minutes or until the peas are mushy.
3 Stir in the sugar and cream and heat through gently. Season to taste with salt and pepper. Sprinkle with parsley to serve.

SERVES 6
PREPARATION & COOKING TIME:
2¹/₂ hours
FREEZING: recommended, after step 5

Grace tells the story of why she makes this soup according to this recipe. 'I once got up at the crack of dawn to visit the famous Parisian market called Les Halles. This no longer exists in Paris – it has moved to an out-of-town location – but I wonder if there are still the little cafés selling onion soup for breakfast? **It was a wonderful experience!** I can't tell you how often I've tried to make onion soup but it never came up to the flavour of the soup I remembered.

'There were the other problems, too, like fighting with a cheesy slice of baguette floating on top! What is the right way to tackle this without using a knife and fork as well? Droopy onions – which refuse to sit in the spoon and often end up trailing down my chin – are something else I dislike. All of these problems are solved in this recipe by my fellow journalist from the Yorkshire Post, the chef, Steven Jackson. This soup is superb: not at all quickly made but worth the effort and expense.'

FOR THE SOUP:
115 g (4 oz) butter
2 kg (4 lb 8 oz) large onions, sliced as thinly as possible, slices cut into short lengths
15 ml (1 tablespoon) plain flour
1.5 litres (2³/₄ pints) rich and jellied beef stock – the best quality you can manage (you could use fresh stock from the super market, or canned consommé)
150 ml (¹/₄ pint) dry white wine
salt and pepper
brandy or Calvados

FOR THE CROÛTES:
1 garlic clove, crushed
50 g (2 oz) butter, softened
5 ml (1 teaspoon) chopped fresh parsley
175 g (6 oz) Gruyère cheese, grated finely
1 small baguette

1 You will need a pan big enough to take all the soup ingredients.
2 First, melt the butter in the pan and add the onions. Stir well and then turn the heat to the lowest setting and cover the onions with a circle of dampened greaseproof paper. Allow the onions to soften for about an hour, stirring frequently.
3 Now remove the paper and turn up the heat. Stir constantly and allow the onions to brown evenly.
4 Sprinkle the flour over the onions and stir and cook this roux for a couple of minutes.
5 Add the stock, a little at a time, stirring without stopping. As the soup thickens, add the wine plus a splash of brandy or Calvados. Allow this to simmer for about a further hour. Check the seasoning.
6 Meanwhile, preheat the oven to 220°C/fan oven 200°C/Gas Mark 7. To make the garlic butter, add the garlic and parsley to the butter and beat well.
7 Cut the bread into enough 2.5 cm (1-inch) thick slices to cover the surface of the soup. Spread the bread with the garlic butter and dip each slice into the grated cheese. Set the bread slices, cheesy-side up, on a baking sheet. Bake for about 10–15 minutes or until the cheese is bubbly and golden. Leave the bread to cool and then break the slices into bite-size pieces.
8 Have ready six fairly large soup bowls that will stand up to being put under a hot grill or in the oven, and warm them up. Check that the soup is very hot and then divide it between the bowls. Then place the cheesy toasts on the surface and sprinkle over the rest of the cheese. Place the bowls under a grill or in the oven and bake or grill until the cheese melts and bubbles. Serve at once.

FRENCH ONION SOUP

SERVES 6
PREPARATION & COOKING TIME:
45 minutes
FREEZING: recommended, after step 8

Both marrow and large courgettes are rather tasteless but blend well with strong flavours. Dilwen originally devised this recipe to use up overgrown courgettes from the garden: the soup is equally delicious hot or chilled.

MARROW & GARLIC SOUP

1 large head of garlic
45 ml (3 tablespoons) oil
1 large onion, chopped
1 marrow, weighing about 1.75 kg (3½ lb)
850 ml (1½ pints) vegetable stock (page 75)
juice of 1 lemon
60 ml (4 tablespoons) chopped fresh parsley
salt and pepper
90 ml (6 tablespoons) cream, to serve

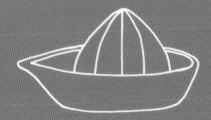

1 Preheat the oven to 200°C/400°F/Gas Mark 6.
2 Break the garlic into cloves. Cut off the root end but do not peel.
3 Toss the cloves in 30 ml (2 tablespoons) of the oil and roast in the oven for about 30 minutes or until the cloves are slightly caramelised. Leave until cool enough to handle.
4 Meanwhile, in a large pan soften the onion in the remaining oil, without browning it.
5 Peel, de-seed, and roughly chop the marrow. Add to the onion.
6 Press the pulp out of the garlic cloves into the marrow mixture. Discard the skins.

7 Add the stock to the marrow mixture, bring to the boil and then reduce the heat and simmer for approximately 20 minutes, or until the marrow is soft.
8 Cool the soup slightly and then reduce to a purée.
9 If serving hot, reheat and stir in the lemon juice and parsley. Adjust the seasoning and serve with a swirl of cream.
10 If serving cold, chill for several hours. Just before serving, add the lemon juice and parsley and check the seasoning. Swirl cream into each serving.

WINTER SOUPS

SERVES 4
PREPARATION TIME:
15 minutes + 1 hour cooking
FREEZING:
recommended, without dumplings

40 g (1½ oz) butter
400 g (12 oz) stewing beef,
trimmed of fat and cubed
1 onion, chopped finely
1 litre (1¾ pints) beef stock (page 76)
450 g (1 lb) mixed root vegetables,
e.g. carrots, swede, parsnips,
turnips, chopped
1 leek, sliced thinly
30 ml (2 tablespoons) chopped fresh parsley
salt and freshly ground black pepper

FOR THE DUMPLINGS:
50 g (2 oz) self-raising flour
15 g (½ oz) suet
5 ml (1 teaspoon) chopped fresh parsley
fresh thyme leaves
salt and pepper
about 10 ml (2 teaspoons) milk

This is a traditional recipe and a **great favourite**, judging by the number of members who suggested using it in the book. It is a complete meal, tasty and very satisfying.

1   Melt half the butter in a pan and quickly fry the beef to seal and brown. Remove the beef with a slotted spoon.
2   Melt the remainder of the butter and fry the onion until golden.
3   Add the stock and beef. Bring to the boil and then reduce the heat and leave to simmer.
4   Meanwhile, prepare the vegetables and then add to the beef. Bring back to the boil and then leave to simmer until the beef and vegetables are tender, about 45–60 minutes.
4   Add the leek and parsley and simmer the soup for a further 5 minutes.
5   Meanwhile, make the dumplings. Mix the flour, suet, herbs and seasoning together in a bowl. Blend together with milk until you have a soft but not sticky dough. Shape into walnut-sized balls by rolling in floury hands.
8   Add the dumplings to the soup and cook for 5 minutes. Turn after 5 minutes and cook for about 5 minutes more. The dumplings will be light and fluffy when cooked.
9   Check and adjust the seasoning of the soup and serve straight away, piping hot.

BEEF SOUP WITH DUMPLINGS

SERVES 6
PREPARATION TIME: 20 minutes + 45 minutes cooking
FREEZING: recommended for the soup, not the croûtes

QUICK ONION SOUP

Traditional French onion soup is fine if you have the time to make it (see page 54). **The recipe below is just as tasty**, provided that the onions are caramelised properly, and it can be served in a non-ovenproof soup dish. Caramelising the onions can be done quickly but take care to keep stirring them, otherwise they will burn.

Dilwen found this a great favourite with her guests when she ran a farm guesthouse.

50 g (2 oz) butter
15 ml (1 tablespoon) olive oil
1.1 kg (2¹/₂ lb) onions, sliced thinly
2.5 ml (¹/₂ teaspoon) demerara sugar
1.1 litres (2 pints) beef stock (page 76)
300 ml (¹/₂ pint) dry white wine
salt and pepper

FOR THE CROÛTES:
6 slices of french bread
175 g (6 oz) Gruyére cheese, grated

1   In a large, thick-based pan, melt the butter with the oil.
2   Add the onions and sugar and cook until golden brown.
    Add 2 tablespoons of the stock if the butter and oil have been absorbed before the all the onions are ready, to prevent the onions from burning.
3   Add the stock and half the wine and bring to the boil. Reduce the heat, cover and simmer for 30–45 minutes.
4   Add the remainder of the wine and adjust the seasoning.
5   Meanwhile, toast the french bread. Cover each slice with grated cheese and place under the grill until the cheese has melted.
6   Pour the soup into individual bowls. Dunk a slice of the cheese-covered french bread into each bowl so the toast absorbs the soup. Serve at once.

SERVES 6
PREPARATION TIME: 20 minutes + 3 hours cooking + chilling overnight + 20 minutes more cooking
FREEZING: recommended

SCOTCH BROTH

Start this recipe the day before you need it, so you can chill the soup overnight and remove every scrap of fat from the top, for the **best flavour**.

900 g (2 lb) scrag end of lamb, trimmed of all excess fat
2 litres (3½ pints) water
115 g (4 oz) pearl barley
a bouquet garni
1 onion, chopped finely
1 small white turnip, diced
2 large carrots, diced, or 2 tablespoons of diced swede
115 g (4 oz) cabbage, shredded
1 large leek, sliced
salt and freshly ground black pepper
15 ml (1 tablespoon) finely chopped fresh parsley, to garnish

1 Place the meat in a large, heavy-based saucepan and add the water, barley and bouquet garni. Season with salt and pepper.
2 Bring the pan slowly to the boil. Skim any white scum from the surface, cover and simmer for 2 hours.
3 Add the onion, turnip and carrot to the soup and continue to simmer for 1 hour.
4 Remove the meat from the soup with a slotted spoon and leave it to stand until it is cool enough to handle. Strip the meat from the bones and cut into small pieces. Cover and reserve.
5 Allow the soup to cool and then chill it overnight, so the fat rises and sets on the surface.
6 Remove the fat. Bring the soup back up to the boil.
7 Return the meat to the soup and add the cabbage and leek. Bring back to the boil, adjust the seasoning and simmer for another 20 minutes.
8 Serve with a sprinkling of chopped parsley.

SERVES 4
PREPARATION TIME: 25 minutes + 30 minutes cooking
FREEZING: recommended

HEARTY WINTER SOUP

This is a substantial soup that is simple to make but very tasty.

575 ml (1 pint) vegetable or chicken stock (page 75 or 77)
1 potato, diced
1 onion, diced
1 large carrot, diced
1 tomato, skinned (page 30) and chopped roughly
1 turnip or half a swede, diced
1 small parsnip, diced
15 ml (1 tablespoon) tomato purée
30 ml (2 tablespoons) chopped fresh parsley
salt and pepper

1 Put the stock into a large saucepan and bring to the boil.
2 Add the vegetables as they are prepared, together with the tomato purée.
3 When it is just at the boil, reduce the heat, cover and simmer gently for about 30 minutes or until the vegetables are tender.
4 Stir in most of the parsley and then check and adjust the seasoning.
5 Serve this soup as it is or let it cool slightly and purée until smooth.
6 Serve sprinkled with the rest of the parsley.

SERVES 4
PREPARATION & COOKING TIME: 15 minutes
FREEZING: recommended

BEAN & TOMATO SOUP

This is a simple, satisfying, tasty soup and was one of the recipes devised when WI members in Wales took part in a health initiative to reduce fat, sugar and salt and increase fibre in their diets.

2 celery sticks, chopped finely
1 small onion, chopped finely
fresh thyme sprig
575 ml (1 pint) vegetable stock (page 75)
400 g can of tomatoes
200 g can of baked beans in tomato sauce
Worcestershire sauce
salt and pepper
chopped fresh parsley, to garnish

1 Cook the celery, onion and thyme in a small amount of stock until tender.
2 Meanwhile, purée the tomatoes and baked beans until smooth.
3 Mix the tomato mixture with the celery and onion; add the remaining stock, a few drops of Worcestershire sauce and seasoning to taste.
4 Remove the sprig of thyme. Bring the soup to the boil and then reduce the heat and leave to simmer for 5 minutes before serving.

SERVES 6
PREPARATION & COOKING TIME: about 30 minutes
FREEZING: recommended

TURKEY NOODLE SOUP

The juices left in the roasting tin after cooking the turkey set to form a jelly. Remove the fat once it has set and use the jellied juices as a delicious stock for this soup, making up the quantity with chicken stock.

1 onion, chopped finely
1.1 litres (2 pints) turkey stock
50 g (2 oz) noodles
225 g (8 oz) cooked turkey, chopped finely
salt and pepper

1 In a large pan, cook the onion in a little of the stock until tender, about 5 minutes.
2 Add the remaining stock and the noodles. Cook following the instructions on the noodle packet.
3 Add the chopped turkey and heat through. Adjust the seasoning.
4 Spoon the noodles into warmed soup bowls, using a slotted spoon. Ladle the soup over the noodles and serve at once.

SERVES 4
PREPARATION TIME: 10 minutes + 15 minutes cooking
FREEZING: not recommended

LEEK & BROCCOLI SOUP

50 g (2 oz) butter
450 g (1 lb) leeks, sliced thinly
225 g (8 oz) broccoli, chopped
1 garlic clove (optional)
30 ml (2 tablespoons) plain flour
575 ml (1 pint) vegetable or chicken stock (page 75 or 77)
575 ml (1 pint) milk
salt and pepper
single cream or crème fraîche, to serve

1 Melt the butter in a large pan and fry the leeks and broccoli, and garlic (if using), for 5 minutes.
2 Sprinkle in the flour, stir well and cook briefly. Then add the stock, make sure all the flour is blended and bring to the boil.
3 Reduce the heat and cook for 15 minutes, or until the vegetables are softened.
4 Allow to cool briefly. Purée if you wish, or leave it chunky.
5 Return to the pan, add the milk and season to taste. Reheat gently, without letting it boil. Serve at once, with a swirl of cream in each bowlful.

SERVES 4–6

PREPARATION TIME: 3–4 hours soaking +
10 minutes + 30 minutes cooking
FREEZING: recommended, after step 4

This is a lovely soup for a cold wintery day, served piping hot with a nice bread roll.

Grace has never managed to preserve fresh mint in a way that she thought did justice to its flavour; dried mint loses its flavour quickly as well, once the jar is opened. In this recipe, however, she uses mint sauce from a jar and it works well.

WINTER LENTIL & MINT SOUP

115 g (4 oz) brown lentils
15 ml (1 tablespoon) oil
a knob of butter
1 onion, sliced finely
1 small garlic clove, sliced
30 ml (2 tablespoons) tomato purée
1.1 litres (2 pints) vegetable
or chicken stock (page 75 or 77)
40 g (1½ oz) bulgar wheat
10 ml (2 teaspoons) lemon juice
10 ml (2 heaped teaspoons) mint sauce
or 30 ml (2 tablespoons)
chopped fresh mint
salt and pepper

1 Put the lentils in a bowl, cover with cold water and leave to soak for 3–4 hours.
2 In a roomy pan, melt the oil and butter together. Add the onion and garlic and cook gently until the onion starts to soften.
3 Drain and rinse the lentils. Stir the tomato purée and drained lentils into the pan and stir so that all is well mixed. Add the stock and bring to the boil.
4 Reduce the heat and leave to simmer for about 30 minutes, or until the lentils are soft.

5 Leave to cool briefly and then spoon out 2 tablespoonfuls of the lentils and set them aside. Purée the soup.
6 Return to the pan and stir in the bulgar wheat, lemon juice and mint sauce or chopped mint. Adjust the seasoning, adding more mint if you wish.
7 Simmer for another 2 minutes. Return the whole lentils to the soup and serve piping hot.

SERVES 6
PREPARATION & COOKING TIME:
25 minutes
FREEZING: recommended, after step 4

This is a recipe Dilwen developed to use up Christmas leftovers. It is easy to make and takes very little cooking. The sweet chestnuts and the sharp cranberries combine to give a delicious flavour and a delicate mushroom-coloured, satisfying, yet low-calorie soup. It can be made at any time during the year, using frozen cranberries and canned or vaccuum-packed chestnuts or unsweetened chestnut purée.

CHESTNUT & CRANBERRY SOUP

If you decide to use fresh chestnuts, skinning them is time-consuming! Puncture each chestnut with a fork, put in a pan of boiling water and keep at simmering point. Remove a few chestnuts at a time and plunge into cold water. Skin with the help of a vegetable knife.

6 shallots, chopped
3 celery sticks, chopped
1 litre (1³/₄ pints) vegetable stock (page 75)
a sprig of thyme
450 g (1 lb) peeled, cooked chestnuts
115 g (4 oz) cranberries
60 ml (4 tablespoons) port
10 ml (2 tablespoons) lemon juice
salt and pepper
celery leaves, to garnish

1 Soften the shallots and celery in 30 ml (2 tablespoons) of stock over a low heat until transparent.
2 Add the remaining stock and thyme. Bring to the boil. Reduce the heat and leave to simmer for 10 minutes.
3 Add the chestnuts and cranberries. Bring to the boil and simmer for a further 5 minutes.
4 Remove the thyme and a few cranberries for the garnish. Allow the soup to cool slightly and then liquidise.
5 Stir in the port and lemon juice to taste. Adjust the seasoning.
6 Reheat gently and serve garnished with cranberries and celery leaves.

CHICKEN PESTO SOUP *pictured opposite*

SERVES 4–6
PREPARATION & COOKING TIME:
30 minutes
FREEZING: recommended, without pesto

15 ml (1 tablespoon) oil
2 chicken leg portions, halved
1 large onion, chopped
30 ml (2 tablespoons) plain flour
1 litre (1¾ pints) chicken stock (page 77)
15 ml (1 tablespoon) tomato purée
80 g (3 oz) pasta shapes, e.g. twists,
shells or quills
225 g (8 oz) broccoli, cut into small florets,
soft part of stalk sliced
115 g (4 oz) french beans, sliced thickly
45 ml (3 tablespoons) pesto sauce
salt and pepper

This is Janet Melvin's recipe. She comments that it is colourful, satisfying and there is only one pan to wash at the end of the meal! This is **a substantial soup**, which can be served as a main course.

1   Heat the oil in a large saucepan and fry the chicken pieces on both sides until browned, about 10 minutes.
2   Add the onion and continue to fry for a further 10 minutes, stirring occasionally.
3   Stir in the flour to combine with the juices.
4   Add the stock and tomato purée and season well. Stir well to make sure the flour is completely blended, bring to the boil, cover and simmer for 15 minutes.
5   Stir in the pasta and cook for 5 minutes.
6   Add the broccoli and beans and cook for a few more minutes, until the vegetables and pasta are tender but not soft.
7   Remove the chicken from the pan. When cool enough to handle, discard the skin and bones and cut the meat into thin strips. Return to the pan, together with the pesto sauce.
8   Stir well, reheat and serve immediately.

LEEK, ONION & POTATO SOUP

SERVES 6
PREPARATION TIME:
25 minutes + 30 minutes cooking
FREEZING:
recommended, without the cream

50 g (2 oz) butter
1 onion, chopped
350 g (12 oz) potatoes, chopped
4 large leeks, sliced
1 litre (1¾ pints) vegetable
or chicken stock (page 75 or 77)
300 ml (½ pint) milk
salt and freshly ground black pepper
90 ml (6 tablespoons) cream, to serve

This is an ever-popular soup. The easiest way to wash leeks is to discard the outer tough layer and then slit the leek from top to root and to the centre and wash under a running tap, holding the root end nearest to the tap, so any grit washes towards the open end.

1   In a large pan, melt the butter and add the onion, potato and leek. Cover the pan with a lid and sweat the vegetables over a low heat for 15 minutes, shaking the pan from time to time.
2   Add the stock, bring to the boil and then reduce the heat and leave to simmer for 15 minutes, until the vegetables are cooked.
3   Add the milk and purée the soup. Return to the pan.
4   Adjust the seasoning and then reheat the soup gently, without boiling.
5   Serve with a swirl of cream in each bowlful.

SERVES 4
PREPARATION TIME: 10 minutes + 30 minutes cooking
FREEZING: recommended

CHICK-PEA & TOMATO SOUP

I think we have all said at one time or another 'What on earth is there to eat?' This soup is a good answer, as it can be made mostly from ingredients in the storecupboard but is nevertheless tasty and satisfying.

30 ml (2 tablespoons) sunflower oil
1 red onion, chopped
2 garlic cloves, crushed
10 ml (2 teaspoons) cumin seeds
5 ml (1 teaspoon) mild curry powder
2 x 400 g (14 oz) cans of chopped tomatoes
175 g (6 oz) carrots, diced
50 g (2 oz) red lentils
finely grated zest and juice of 1 orange
425 g can of chick-peas, drained
salt and freshly ground black pepper
croûtons, to serve (page 23)

1 Heat the oil in a large pan and cook the onion, garlic, cumin seeds and curry powder for 5 minutes.
2 Add the tomatoes, carrots, lentils and orange zest to the pan. Then make up the orange juice to 575 ml (1 pint) with water and stir into the soup. Bring to the boil, cover and simmer for 30 minutes, until the carrots are tender.
3 Meanwhile, make the croûtons (page 23), and keep warm.
4 Allow the soup to cool briefly. Purée the soup or use a potato masher to give a fairly coarse texture. Then toss in the chick-peas and season to taste.
5 Reheat the soup and serve with the croûtons.

SERVES 4
PREPARATION & COOKING TIME: 50 minutes
FREEZING: recommended

CAWL CENNIN (LEEK BROTH)

A traditional Welsh dish, this is often served with bread and cheese for a light but well balanced meal. The leek is, of course, one of the Welsh emblems proudly worn on Saint David's Day, March 1st. It has a delicate onion flavour, is easy to grow and is available for ten months of the year.

50 g (2 oz) butter
2 onions, chopped
225 g (8 oz) mixed root vegetables, e.g. carrots, parsnips, turnips and swede, diced
1.1 litres (2 pints) vegetable stock (page 75)
2 large leeks, sliced thinly
15 ml (1 tablespoon) chopped fresh parsley
salt and pepper

1 In a large pan, melt the butter and sauté the onions and root vegetables for 15 minutes, without browning.
2 Add the stock, bring to the boil and then reduce the heat and simmer for 15 minutes.
3 Add the leeks and parsley and cook for a further 10 minutes.
4 Adjust the seasoning before serving.

SERVES 4
PREPARATION & COOKING TIME: 50 minutes
FREEZING: recommended

VEGETABLE CHOWDER

15 ml (1 tablespoon) oil
1 large onion, chopped
225 g (8 oz) potatoes, chopped
225 g (8 oz) carrots, diced
3 celery sticks, diced
400 g (14 oz) can of chopped tomatoes
115 g (4 oz) macaroni
425 ml ($^3/_4$ pint) vegetable stock (page 75)
1 bay leaf
10 ml (2 teaspoons) dried oregano
300 ml ($^1/_2$ pint) milk
salt and freshly ground black pepper
chopped fresh parsley, to garnish

1 Heat the oil in a large saucepan. Add the onion, potatoes, carrots and celery and sauté for 5 minutes, stirring occasionally.
2 Add the tomatoes, pasta, stock and herbs. Bring to the boil, reduce the heat, cover and simmer for 15 minutes.
3 Stir in the milk and season to taste. Bring back to the boil and then discard the bay leaf.
4 Serve sprinkled with chopped parsley.

SERVES 5–6
PREPARATION & COOKING TIME: 20 minutes + 2 hours chilling
FREEZING: recommended, before adding milk or cream

WATERCRESS, ORANGE & ALMOND SOUP

2 bunches of fresh, perky watercress, thoroughly washed
    and patted dry
15 ml (1 tablespoon) oil
1 small onion, chopped finely
850 ml (1$^1/_2$ pints) vegetable or chicken stock (page 75 or 77)
30 ml (2 tablespoons) ground almonds
juice of 1 sweet orange
5 ml (1 teaspoon) grated orange zest
300 ml ($^1/_2$ pint) mixed milk and single cream
salt and pepper
6 whole almonds, skinned, chopped and toasted, to garnish

1 Pick over the watercress, removing any yellow leaves. Reserve a few small leaves to garnish.
2 Heat the oil in a roomy pan and cook the onion, without browning. When the onion is soft, add the stock, ground almonds and watercress. Season to taste. Simmer for just a few minutes.
3 Stir the orange juice and zest into the soup. Simmer for another 3–4 minutes only.
4 Allow to cool and then reduce the soup to a smooth purée. Stir in the milk and cream mixture.
5 Allow the soup to cool and then refrigerate it for 2 hours.
6 Check the seasoning. Serve in small bowls – it should be chilled but not icy. Sprinkle a few chopped toasted almonds on top of each bowl of soup, along with the reserved watercress leaves.

SERVES 4
PREPARATION TIME: 35 minutes + 20 minutes cooking
FREEZING: recommended

The pinkish colour of the sweet potato and deep red of the pepper give this soup a delightful colour and the coconut milk adds a tropical flavour.

25 g (1 oz) butter
1 onion, chopped
1 garlic clove, crushed
15 ml (1 tablespoon) ground coriander
450 g (1 lb) sweet potato, grated
2 red peppers, chopped
700 ml (1¼ pints) vegetable stock (page 75)
400 g can of coconut milk

SWEET POTATO & RED PEPPER SOUP

WITH COCONUT

1 Melt the butter in a large pan. Add the onion and garlic and cook over a low heat until soft.
2 Stir in the ground coriander and cook for 2 minutes.
3 Add the sweet potato and red pepper to the pan and cook for 5 minutes.
4 Pour the vegetable stock over and bring to the boil; cover and simmer for 20 minutes.
5 Allow to cool a little and then purée.
6 Return to the rinsed-out pan and add the coconut milk. Heat gently until piping hot and then serve at once.

NOTE: If coconut milk isn't available, use 100 g (3½ oz) of creamed coconut, chopped, and increase the amount of stock by about 150 ml (¼ pint).

SERVES 4
PREPARATION & COOKING TIME:
20 minutes
FREEZING: recommended

This is a modern version of boiled bacon and cabbage, a perennial favourite. It is quick and easy to make, looks good and tastes even better!

25 g (1 oz) butter
2 onions, chopped finely
6 rashers of rindless bacon, chopped
1 litre (1¾ pints) vegetable stock (page 75)
450 g (1 lb) savoy cabbage, sliced thinly
salt and pepper

CABBAGE &

BACON SOUP

1 Melt the butter in a large pan and soften the onion over a low heat, without browning.
2 Add the bacon and increase the heat. Stirring continuously, cook until the onions and bacon begin to brown.
3 Add the stock and bring to the boil.
4 Add the cabbage. Cook until the cabbage is tender but still firm, approximately 5 minutes.
5 Adjust the seasoning before serving.

SERVES 4
PREPARATION TIME:
10 minutes + 15 minutes cooking
FREEZING: recommended

15 ml (1 tablespoon) olive oil
25 g (1 oz) butter
1 onion, chopped
450 g (1 lb) carrots, chopped
225 g (8 oz) apples, chopped
875 ml (1½ pints) vegetable stock (page 75)
salt and pepper
freshly grated nutmeg, to serve

CARROT &
APPLE SOUP

1 Heat the oil and butter in a large pan until the butter has melted. Add the onion and chopped carrot and apple. Cover the pan and sweat the vegetables for 5 minutes, shaking the pan from time to time.
2 Add the stock and cook for 15 minutes, or until the vegetables are tender.
3 Allow to cool slightly and then reduce to a purée.
4 Adjust the seasoning. Reheat and serve with a sprinkling of nutmeg.

SERVES 6
PREPARATION & COOKING TIME: 50 minutes
FREEZING: not recommended

15 ml (1 tablespoon) oil
1 onion, chopped
2 large potatoes, chopped
1.1 litres (2 pints) vegetable or chicken stock (page 75 or 77)
350 g (12 oz) broccoli, chopped roughly
80 g (3 oz) Stilton cheese, crumbled
150 ml (5 fl oz) milk
salt, pepper and juice of ½ lemon
90 ml (6 tablespoons) cream, to serve

BROCCOLI &
STILTON SOUP

1 Heat the oil in a fairly large pan and soften the onion for a few minutes. Add the potatoes and stock and bring to the boil. Simmer for 10 minutes.
2 Add the broccoli and cook for further 10 minutes. Purée the soup or just mash the vegetables roughly, if you prefer a chunkier texture.
3 Add the Stilton and milk and season to taste with salt, pepper and lemon juice. Heat through, without boiling.
4 Serve with a swirl of cream in each bowl.

SERVES 6
PREPARATION TIME:
30 minutes + 20 minutes cooking
FREEZING:
recommended for the soup, not the salsa

Sîan Cook submitted this recipe. She says: '**It is a hot, spicy soup and the salsa is a cooling complement**. The colour is vibrant and the younger generation love it.'
Dilwen found the older generation enjoyed it too!

FOR THE SOUP:
30 ml (2 tablespoons) oil
2 onions, chopped
4 fat garlic cloves, crushed
10 ml (2 teaspoons) ground cumin
a pinch of cayenne pepper
15 ml (1 tablespoon) paprika
15 ml (1 tablespoon) tomato purée
30 ml (2 tablespoons) ground coriander
400 g can of chopped tomatoes
400 g can of red kidney beans, drained
1 litre (1³/₄ pints) vegetable stock (page 75)
salt and pepper

FOR THE SALSA:
2 avocados, chopped
1 red onion, chopped finely
1 green chilli, de-seeded and chopped finely
15 ml (1 tablespoon) chopped fresh coriander
juice of 1 lime

1   Heat the oil in a large saucepan and cook the onion and garlic until softened.
2   Add all the remaining ingredients for the soup, bring to the boil, season and cook over a low heat for 20 minutes.
3   Meanwhile, mix the salsa ingredients together.
4   Leave the soup to cool briefly. Then purée the soup and return to the pan. Adjust the seasoning and reheat gently.
5   Serve a little salsa in the middle of each bowl of soup.

SPICY BEAN SOUP WITH GUACAMOLE SALSA

STOCKS

Not long ago, the chef-restaurateur and television presenter Brian Turner gave a demonstration to the Guild of Food Writers, of which Grace is a member. This was no glamorous meal of such enormous complexity as to **dazzle** us all.

We were dazzled, though, because he showed us how stock was made – and still is, at quality restaurants – in the classic tradition. He took us through all the stages and let us taste the liquid as it improved and improved. Even vegetable stock was triumphantly tasty!

Brian used huge, vat-like pans from his restaurant in Walton Street in London. He showed us what went into the stock, the vegetables, the bouquets garnis, the veal bones and fish bones. In true TV tradition, he had to have his stock at different stages (prepared earlier) so that we could appreciate the flavours. Long, slow cooking, skimming and de-greasing were all part of it. Then the liquid was strained, cooled quickly, and the remaining fat was lifted from the top. At this point the liquid was reheated and cooked again in open pans, to reduce the quantity and strengthen the flavour.

The longer the reduction process goes on, the stronger the flavour is. Funnily enough, a common complaint at classy restaurants now is that the sauces are too powerfully flavoured from over-reduced stock.

Brian's demonstration was superb. It must have taken ages to prepare and he showed us more clearly than ever why good stock is best.

I do make stock but not in vast quantities and the Fagin-like feeling of satisfaction of getting something for nothing never leaves me. The stock pot of long ago, which had to be brought up to the boil every day, has long gone but, once you learn how to make stock on a small scale and store it for future use, you will never throw out a chicken carcass again!

I do also use stock cubes and bouillon powder. It is fair to say that the best is expensive, however, you can often use just half of the stated amount on the label. It is up to you to taste the dish and see. Fresh stock is also to be had now, in supermarket chill cabinets. This is extremely good but also expensive. Remember that stock cubes and granules contain a percentage of salt. Read the labels carefully and adjust the salt in the recipe.

When making your own stock, it is important to cool it as quickly as possible by sitting the pan in a sink of cold water until it is cool enough to go in the fridge. The stock can be easily frozen for future use and is best if it is used within three months. Freeze it as soon as possible and label carefully with type of stock and the date of making.

The reduction process is often needed to strengthen flavour in a stock or just to reduce the quantity of liquid by half so that it takes up less room in the freezer. The quickest way is to use a wide pan with the lid off over a moderate heat.

Do not season stock when you make it. Salt and pepper are best added when you are ready to use the stock for soups and sauces.

A point I must touch on is how do you know if stock, or anything else for that matter, has gone off? Your sense of smell will tell you if something has started to ferment. The biggest tell-tale sign is when the soup, sauce or stew is cold but a continuous stream of tiny bubbles rise and break on the surface. This is throw-out time.

A pressure cooker can be used to make stock but it will need to be done in two batches. Check the manufacturer's instructions. Likewise, a microwave cooker can be used and of course the smells are kept to a minimum – a bonus in a small kitchen.

VEGETABLE STOCK

FISH STOCK

MAKES about 1.1 litres (2 pints)
PREPARATION TIME: 15 minutes + 40 minutes cooking
FREEZING: recommended

You can use whatever vegetables you have to make stock, adding any herbs which you are fond of. Grace particularly likes the addition of a lemon and she has been known to use some bottled lemon juice instead if she doesn't have a lemon.

1.1 litres (2 pints) cold water
1 small lemon, scrubbed and chopped roughly
1 thick stalk of celery, chopped
2 carrots, chopped
1 onion, chopped
5 ml (1 teaspoon) peppercorns
fresh herbs, e.g. parsley stalks, small bay leaf and sprig of thyme
   (or ¹/₂ teaspoon dried thyme)
1 small garlic clove, sliced (optional)

1   Put everything into a large pan. Bring to the boil and then reduce the heat and leave to simmer for about 30–40 minutes. Any scum which rises should be skimmed off and discarded. A large spoon pulled at an angle across the surface will do it. Leave the lid of the pan at an angle. This prevents the stock from boiling over and also helps to reduce the volume and increase the flavour.
2   Strain the stock through a fine sieve and taste it. You may wish to reduce it further to strengthen the flavour. Simmer in an open pan until you are happy with the taste.
3   Use for soups or sauces or freeze for future use. Remember to label carefully stating type of stock and date. Season the stock when you use it.

MAKES about 1.1 litres (2 pints)
PREPARATION TIME: 10 minutes + 25 minutes cooking
FREEZING: recommended

This is very quick to make and you can save white fish bones in the freezer or you can ask your fishmonger for some. It is best to order the bones in advance so that you get only white bones. Dry white wine gives it a lovely flavour.

900 g (2 lb) white fish bones, rinsed
2 glasses of dry white wine
1.7 litres (3 pints) water
115 g (4 oz) white closed-cup mushrooms, sliced
1 small onion, sliced
parsley stalks and tarragon leaves
5–6 peppercorns

1   Put everything into a large pan. Bring to the boil and then reduce the heat and leave to simmer gently for only 20 minutes.
2   Strain and taste. Carry on reducing the volume until you have a flavoursome liquid, if you wish.
3   Use or freeze for future use. Remember to label carefully, stating type of stock and date of making.
4   Season the stock when you use it.

BEEF STOCK

MAKES about 1.1 litres (2 pints)
PREPARATION TIME: 15 minutes + 3½ hours cooking
FREEZING: recommended

Meat stock needs to be dark in colour.

It used to be made from marrow bones

which we bought raw from the butchers.

We would have the bones cut up for us

so that they would fit into the pan!

Grace's preferred brown stock nowadays is made from the remains of the Sunday rib of beef. She collects them in the freezer and, when she has enough, roasts them again in the oven along with some vegetables. This intensifies the flavour and colour. A fair substitute for home-made beef stock is a can of consommé, which you can dilute a bit to extend it.

1.3 kg (3 lb) beef bones from cooked joints
2 onions, topped and tailed and each cut into 4 (save the skin)
2–3 celery sticks, chopped
2 large carrots, chopped
10 whole black peppercorns
fresh herbs, e.g. parsley stalks, small bay leaf and sprig of thyme
   (or 2.5 ml / ½ teaspoon dried thyme)
1.7 litres (3 pints) cold water

1   First of all, turn the oven to its highest setting. Pack the bones into a large roasting tin. Push all the vegetables in with them and roast for about 45 minutes, by which time the bones should have darkened and the vegetables will have softened and scorched just a little.
2   Move all the contents of the tin into a big pan. Add the onion skins, peppercorns, herbs and water. Add some of the water (or a glass of red wine, if you have one, to the tin and stir vigorously to deglaze the tin and pick up all the flavour. Add the deglazed liquid to the pan.
3   Bring to the boil then reduce the heat and leave to simmer for about 2½ hours. Remove quickly any scum which rises to the surface. Keep the lid on but at an angle.
4   Strain the liquid through a fine sieve, taste it and decide if you want to reduce the stock more.
5   Use or freeze for future use, removing any fat that rises to the surface during cooling before freezing. Label carefully with the type of stock and date of making. Season only when you are going to use it

CHICKEN STOCK

MAKES about 1.1 litres (2 pints)
PREPARATION TIME: 10 minutes + 2½ hours cooking
FREEZING: recommended

Chicken is probably the most useful of all stocks.

It's a good idea to freeze chicken carcasses until you gather sufficient together to make a batch of stock. You can also include skin and jelly left behind after carving. Break the carcasses up a bit to fit into your pan.

The colour of this stock is quite light. To make a darker stock, first fry the broken carcasses in oil until they are brown. You can also sear the onion by cutting it in two and frying the cut sides until almost burnt. The resulting stock will be much darker after this treatment. The addition of a glass of dry white wine or even brandy gives another dimension to the flavour. Tarragon is one of Grace's favourite herbs for adding to this stock.

2 large chicken carcasses or 3 smaller ones
1 large onion, sliced
2 celery sticks, chopped
1 large carrot, chopped
fresh herbs, e.g. parsley talks, sprig of thyme,
    bay leaf and sprig of tarragon
1 fat garlic clove, chopped (optional)
10 black peppercorns
1.1 litres (2 pints) cold water

1   Put all the ingredients in a large pan and bring to the boil; then reduce the heat and leave to simmer for about 2–2½ hours. Whisk away any scum which rises to the surface and discard it. Refrain from boiling hard as this can make the stock cloudy.
2   Pour through a fine sieve. Taste the stock to check its strength. Reduce it in a clean pan with the lid off, if you wish.
3   Cool the stock overnight in the fridge and the following day you will be able to remove any fat from the surface. The stock is then ready to use or freeze for future use. Label carefully with type of stock and the date of making.
4   Season when about to use.